"Richard Hardy nailed it! *Transformational Management and Leadership* is sure to be a hit with leaders, and managers alike. Very informative and helpful. A must-read!"

Steve Vicari
Executive Director of Men's Development
Homes of Hope, Inc.

"This book is a 'Must-Read Guide' for anyone running a small business or managing any team of employees, regardless of the size. Whether you're managing a few people or hundreds, Rick's no-nonsense applications of leadership and team-building are invaluable. His first-hand experience and simple yet profound insight make this book a necessity for anyone striving to build a winning team. Truly one of the best leadership books I have read in my 25 years in business."

Bill Hutchinson
Owner/President
Hutchinson Publishing Corp./Green Source Direct, Inc.

"I have worked with Rick for over 20 years. During that time, I have watched him grow from a novice nurse into an exemplary leader. The principles of leadership developed by Rick over the past 20 years provide a practical, "real world" foundation to transform your management practices. This book will give every leader the tools to become an inspirational leader. These principles are highly effective as I have had the opportunity to witness the transformation of multiple groups under Rick's leadership."

Joyce Griffin RN, BSN, CCRN
Nurse Manager
Neuro-Trauma ICU, Greenville Memorial Medical Campus

"When his team struggled, Rick dared to look in the mirror. He shares what he found and goes beyond concepts and gives the reader practical, how-to advice. Fun and easy to read."

Mike Osler
Regional Director, Proaxis Therapy

"If you desire to change the culture of your business in a positive and productive way, then this is the book for you. Having Rick as a best friend since the seventh grade gave me the benefit of hearing his voice as I read the pages of his book. Knowing him personally and knowing his background gives me even more insight. When he mentions his poor upbringing, it is no exaggeration. However, you would never know this from being around him. This makes Rick's message of self-reliance more meaningful and his unwillingness to make excuses an example for all to follow. As I continue the struggle to work on the culture in our business, a Certified Public Accounting firm, I plan to incorporate many aspects I learned from his book.

Barrett A. Burns
Partner, Morrison & Smith, LLP CPA's

"Proven principles for that next step in taking your team to the next level from a leader who has tested and lived the concepts he writes."

Marian McVey
Chief Nursing Office, North Greenville Medical Campus

"The book has great insight for developing personal leadership skills and for sharing these ideals in a very positive way!"

Gordon Lewis
President, NuChoice Communications, Inc.

"As Rick's lifelong friend and former teammate, you need to know *Transformational Management and Leadership*. It is a well-written book that has ideas and concepts that can endure forever. Most assuredly, these are the ones that you have been looking for. If you are looking to engage and invest in the futures of those you work beside, then this is the book for you. It is filled with unique, hard-hitting examples, along with clearly laid out steps and explanations to make it happen for you. After reading Rick's book, I have been left with a question that will guide me for a long time, 'Why do we do what we do?' This is the question we all need to ask ourselves. He states, 'I am convinced that one cannot change an environment or provide the leadership to change that environment if that individual is not motivated to change it.' Thank you, Rick!"

Timothy B. Eads
Ad Director, Northport Gazette News

Transformational Management and Leadership

*Changing Perspectives, Attitudes, and Performance in
You and Your Organization*

Richard A. Hardy

High Bridge Books
Houston

To my wife, Judy.
You are the sunshine in my life that makes life worth living.

CONTENTS

INTRODUCTION

Why write this book? That is a good question, but to understand the reason I wrote this book, you first have to know the question I could not answer during a critical time of my leadership and managerial career. The question was simply, "If you're such a great manager, then why is your staff not performing up to standards?" This was a question I found myself asking over and over again without an answer. It caused such great frustration within me that it became an obsession. This obsession put me on a path to find the answer.

You see, I had been in many different leadership positions during my career. Not meaning to sound arrogant, but during that time, I had a lot of success without really meeting failure. They say the true character of a person can be seen in how they handle failure rather than how they handle success. Well... I was facing my first real test with failure. It was staring me straight in the face, and I was not handling it very well.

It was during this time of struggle that I faced my failure as a leader. I had to take a long hard look at the person staring back at me in the mirror. The resulting revelation and transformation would not only change my leadership and managerial philosophy, but it would also change the relationships I had with colleagues and staff. It would change my view of life and change the course of my career.

It was such a great transformation that it inspired me to write this book for those in leadership positions who are caught in the same situation in which I had found myself.

The principles contained herein work! I know because I've done it with a staff as small as 14 and one as large as 120 — with incredible results.

If you are working harder than ever before with seemingly worse results, unable to break free from the cycle of apathy and frustration and unable to answer the question that I could not answer, then I would encourage you to read this book. I believe with all my heart that it will change the Perspective, Attitude, and Performance of not only you but also those you lead!

To change a culture, an attitude, or an environment, one must have a vision, a belief in that vision, and must act upon that belief. Only through a sincerity of change that comes from within will a true commitment produce the desired change.

CHAPTER 1

A STORY OF APATHY AND AWAKENING

In order to understand why I wrote this book, I have to go back and explain the situation in which I found myself several years ago. During that time, I was becoming increasingly frustrated with the level of performance from my staff. I was managing a staff of 14 and had been doing so for quite some time. My managerial style was laissez-faire because the quality of my staff was of the highest caliber.

During this time, I started witnessing a decline in their work product. As this was occurring, I was engaging only to correct it. The more I engaged to correct performance, the more their work product declined, as well as their morale.

Over time, I became more and more involved and engaged — with worsening results. I utilized everything within my experience and knowledge to turn things around. Techniques I had success with in the past were not working. I also engaged in coaching sessions and one-on-one meetings with individual staff members. I sought advice from colleagues and had conversations with my boss to resolve the issue. I gave written as well as oral tests, checking for competency. I even held a retreat for the staff. Looking back, I managed to mess that up, too! The problem was, the more I became involved, the worse the results became.

It culminated with my department being involved in a couple of decisions that reached all the way up the corporate ladder. In other words, it wasn't good. To say I was frustrated would be an understatement. As I became more involved and engaged, the more pressure I brought upon the staff. Apathy was running rampant, and morale was low.

My view was that my staff was not responding. *They* did not get it, I reasoned. We found ourselves in a vicious downward-spiral regarding performance. Things were falling apart, and I didn't have the answers any longer. We were not adding value to the organization, and I was at a loss, looking for a break. I was looking for answers, and there were none to be found.

MOMENT OF DECISION

During this time of declining performance, I had been holding regular monthly sessions with my boss, Carol Moody. She is, without a doubt, one of the best leaders I have ever worked for. I say that not because I am including her in this book but because she understands leadership. She knows how to influence without micro-managing, how to be supportive without removing responsibility, how to instill confidence, and how to set expectations without being punitive. Last but not least, she knows how to inspire!

Carol didn't try to tell me how to run my department. She was supportive, and when we would meet, it was an environment of total honesty. This would be the key to the process yet to come. During one of these sessions, I realized I had finally become sick of the current environment within our department. Actually, I was sick of being sick! I had what some refer to as an "Ah Ha moment."

During a one-on-one session with Carol, I told her we were going to change the culture within our department and improve performance, come hell or high water! She asked me how I was going to do it, and I remember just sitting there, staring at her blankly and responding, "I have no idea, but it's going to change!"

During this whole episode of decline and after the meeting with Carol, one question seemed to haunt me over and over again. The question was a simple one, yet I didn't yet have an answer for it. The question was, "If you're such a great manager, then why is your staff not performing up to standards?" This question was killing me. I'll say it again: this question was absolutely killing me!

I was facing failure, and I wasn't handling it very well. I was frustrated, angry, and knew things had to change. There is an old saying, "If you can't change the people, then change the people." I have to admit that this thought was also running through my mind. More on this later.

> *"If you are such a great manager, then why isn't your staff performing up to standards?"*

I had been in management at that time for approximately 18 years and had success after success, never really meeting failure. I had been to all of the management seminars, the in-services, and the classes put on by the hospital where I worked. I was seen by many as a resource for new managers. In fact, you could not really tell me much about managing people. You may say that is arrogant, and you know what? It is! I was at the top of my game — at least, I thought so. I didn't realize that my success over the years had produced such a momentum that I could not recognize it was actually my biggest stumbling block. As we progress, you will see why.

MOMENT OF TRUTH – A HAUNTING QUESTION

I made the decision to change the environment in our department, and I believed this was the best way to improve performance. The next step was to share it with the staff. Why did I feel so strongly that changing the environment was the best way to deal with the problem? Intuition is the only thing I can come up with.

> *I will never forget that October staff meeting, because looking back on it, it was the first time, truth be known, in over two years that the staff and I were on the same page.*

I was not reading any books at the time and had not been to an in-service or seminar in a long, long time — probably in years. I knew I wasn't happy, my boss wasn't happy, and corporate wasn't happy. Who can perform in such an unhappy environment?

Seeing that I had nothing left to lose, I decided to hit the problem head on and let the chips fall where they may. Somewhat out of desperation and largely out of determination, I came up with the following plan.

I will never forget that October staff meeting because, looking back on it, it was the first time in over two years that the staff and I were on the same page. I now look back and wonder how I let it get to that point. I started out asking each staff member to tell me if they were happy with their work environment. It was a question I already knew the answer to, but it was important that each member verbalize it. Each staff member did indeed confirm what I thought to be true.

I told them that I totally agreed with their assessment. I then drew a line on a dry erase board and labeled one end, "Apathy," and the other, "Engagement." I asked each staff member to go up to the board and mark where they thought our department was performing. I was not surprised when they all marked on the "Apathy" side of the line. I then explained to the staff my frustration with how things were going in the department and that I was sick of the environment. I shared with them that I was so sick and tired of being sick and tired that we were going to change the environment. I also shared that I didn't think everyone was going to make it.

This got the staff's attention because I'm sure they could see the determination on my face. My boss, Carol, was also there to show her support for the decision. I then told the staff that I wanted them to put themselves in my position and write a plan for how *they* would manage the department.

I then explained that I would use their input to put together a departmental plan of action. I assured them that as I read their plans, I would take off my manager's cap, and there would be no retaliation on my part. They had evaluations coming up in November, and I told them that they could hand in their plans after their annual evaluations.

What they may or may not have known at the time is they were actually giving me a referendum on my management and leadership of the department. It would be an eye-opening exercise, one that I would highly recommend. I will warn you that unless you have thick skin, you may want to consider forgoing this exercise. What your people say will convict your soul and will point out your obvious flaws and mistakes. If you're truly serious about changing the environment, then I highly recommend it. It was genuinely humbling.

Before we left the staff meeting, we all came to an agreement that we wanted to have a department in which we enjoyed working, one of which we could all be proud. We also made a decision that, when we left the meeting, we all had to leave what was in the past in the past. Again, I personally went to each employee and asked if they could wipe the slate clean, let go of the past, and move forward.

This was an important step in gaining total agreement. By verbalizing it in front of the entire group, it carried with it more meaning even if some didn't really mean it. In his book, *Developing the Leader Within You*, John C. Maxwell states, "The greatest day in your life and mine is when we take total responsibility for our attitudes. That's the day we truly grow up."[1]

I had made a decision and asked for their input to help change the department's culture and environment, but the fact still remained: I did not have a plan. General George Patton once said, "When in doubt, go on the offensive," and this was exactly what I intended to do!

REVELATIONS AND AWAKENING

During that same year, I had the pleasure of working with a woman by the name of Laurie Mooney. She was a staffing specialist at our hospital, and I worked with her during times of reallocating staff. Laurie was simply the most positive person I had ever met. Regardless of the situation or the changing of events, Laurie always seemed to put a positive spin on things.

A phrase that comes to mind when I think of Laurie is, "Well… we'll just have to make lemonade out of lemons." While I worked with her, I was intrigued and amazed by her resilience. Because of her positive attitude, she always offered cheer. You always came away feeling good for having interacted with her. I kept wondering what her secret was. I mean, here I am struggling and frustrated as can be, and there she is, handling each obstacle with a superior, positive attitude. Nothing seemed to faze her. What was her secret? I just had to know!

One Sunday afternoon, Laurie brought the staffing books into my office. I finally decided to see if she would divulge her secret. I said, "Laurie, I've been watching you, and I have to say that you are the most positive person I have ever met. Why?" What she said was tremendous.

She told me that it wasn't always so. She said that, at one point, she was probably one of the most unhappy people you'd ever come across. She said that, one day, when she was living in Los Angeles, she became so sick of being unhappy that she decided she was not going to live like that any longer. She made a decision that day to be happy.

She went on to explain that it did not happen overnight, but she was determined that whenever something went wrong, she would make the effort to put a positive spin on it. Over the years, she finally noticed that her whole attitude had changed, and she was now a happy person. I remember noticing the intensity in her facial expressions as she recounted her journey. The determination was obvious, and as she brought herself back to the present, her expression softened, and a big smile appeared on her face.

> *She said that, one day, when she was living in Los Angeles, she became so sick of being unhappy that she decided she was not going to live like that any longer. She made a decision that day to be happy.*

I knew then that I had heard something special, important, and profound. Still, I struggled to put it into perspective—at least, as it pertained to me. Little did I know, this conversation would affect me down the road and would be a part of my own amazing transformation. I will always be grateful to Laurie for sharing her experience with me. It has made a tremendous impact on my life.

What Laurie had stumbled across out of frustration is what Andy Andrews refers to in *The Traveler's Gift: Seven Decisions that Determine Personal Success* as the 5th decision: "Today I will choose to be happy."[2] He puts it in the context of having a grateful spirit. Looking back on my conversations with Laurie, I can see that she did indeed possess a grateful spirit.

Could this be the secret to the happiness she displayed day in and day out? Could this be what I was lacking, which was causing my poisoned perspective and damaged relationships? You see, I didn't know anything about Andy Andrews or the impact he would also have on my life. I also did not know the way in which I would meet Mr. Andrews, but stay tuned!

To my surprise, almost every member of my staff submitted a plan of how they would manage our department. As I stated earlier, it was quite humbling. Over the next several months, I had two more revelations that totally turned my world around. I am not sure of the time frame or sequence of events, but I do know that I was struggling with putting all of this together into a coherent plan of action.

Then, it came to me one evening in a vision. Yep, just as sure as I'm sitting here, I'm telling you the truth. It came to me in a vision! Okay, so I was sitting in the La-Z-Boy, watching TV. Actually, I was watching the Dave Ramsey Show, which was showing at that time on the Fox Business channel. He stated that he had a guest by the name of John G. Miller, author of *QBQ! The Question Behind the Question: Practicing Personal Accountability at Work and in Life*. A light bulb went off inside my head, and I said to myself, "Yes, that's what my staff needs to read."

I watched the interview intently and still did not get it! My focus was still on blaming the staff for the problems of our department. I went out the next day, bought his book, and read it. A curious thing happened while reading it. I had the blinders removed from my brain and realized, "Hoss, the problem with the department was not your staff; it was looking back at you in the mirror each morning!"

That moment was so demoralizing and sobering yet so freeing and exhilarating. It was at that time that I was freed from the ball and chain of past successes and became open to the exciting prospects of a new future.

You may ask, "Why was so freeing and liberating?" It was liberating because it presented a problem I could solve. Because it was me who was the problem, I had no doubt that I would succeed in changing what needed to be changed. It also removed me from the victim mentality of having a staff that was not performing up to my expectations. This gave me control of my own destiny! It gave me hope which I believe is the basis of success.

> *That moment was so demoralizing and sobering yet so freeing and exhilarating. It was at that time that I was freed from the ball and chain of past successes and became open to the exciting prospects of a new future.*

I then took the book to Rhonda Miller, one of my senior staff members and asked if she would read it and give me some feedback. She did and thought it was great. She also thought all of the staff should read it. I knew then that it would be an integral part of the plan to change our environment and culture.

Now that I had the light bulb turned on, I still knew I did not have all I needed to pull it off. I was still missing something, but I could not put my finger on it.

Then, I had another vision! Yep, you guessed it. I was back in the La-Z-Boy, watching Dave Ramsey again. This time, he was interviewing Andy Andrews about his new book, *Mastering the Seven Decisions that Determine Personal Success.*

What caught my attention was listening to Mr. Andrews explain about people who think that life just couldn't get any worse. What he said shocked me. He said, "They're right!" In fact, I sat up in the chair and listened intently on what followed.

He explained how people who are this negative cause other people to avoid them. In the process, they are closing doors of opportunities for their own success. He used the example of when you ask someone how they are doing, and they go on to rant and rave about how bad life is. To them, life just couldn't get any worse. The next time you see them, you start to avoid them. If you are avoiding them, then who else is avoiding them?

This struck a nerve with me. Reflecting back on my own behavior, I knew I had been making almost everyone I came in contact with miserable, and I'm sure people were avoiding me. Maybe... just maybe, my difficulty was coming from my own negative attitude. I then decided to read his book, and I ordered it the next day.

I read Mr. Andrew's book and went through the exercises contained therein. I have to admit it was one of the most difficult things I have done, but as I read and concentrated on the exercises, I started to gain a new perspective. By the time I had finished the book, I had a whole different attitude regarding how I viewed myself, how I viewed my staff, and how I viewed my job. Combined with the other two revelations, I now felt I had a foundation to build and act upon.

I was confident this would produce the change in me that was necessary for changing the environment and culture within our department. It also gave me a whole new perspective on how to interpret the plans my staff had previously handed in. As I re-read their plans, my plan of action materialized before my very eyes. I then knew what I had to do. The vision was there. The staff had painted the picture for me, and I now developed an action plan covering 0-3 months, 3-6 months, and 6-12 months. I planned to kick it off at the end of January at our monthly staff meeting.

> *Maybe… just maybe, my difficulty was coming from my own negative attitude.*

"New Beginnings" is what I named our staff meetings. I changed locations and format. Most importantly, I changed my way of conducting them. We shortened them, and I provided the positive energy and direction needed to start moving that heavy wheel of apathy towards engagement.

My staff thought that I had gone absolutely crazy! I remember looking into their faces, seeing the look of shock and confusion as to what they were witnessing. Their laughs were nervous ones of disbelief. Their claps were as if they were at a golf tournament, but their excitement grew as the meeting went along.

I could also sense a sigh of relief. It wasn't an audible sigh but one observed through the staff members' newly relaxed countenances and increasingly confident smiles. At this time, I knew I was on the right path. As with all new initiatives, I knew they would be watching me to see if this was a one-time thing or whether or not I had truly changed. I knew this and had committed to this new path. Only through consistency of action would the confidence be instilled to create the momentum of change we all desired.

I will never forget that night because after the meeting, one of my staff members (Teresa Brown) came up to me. While pinching my arm, she asked if it was really me. It was a special moment and one that stays with me until this day. Over the next month, the whole staff voluntarily read *QBQ*, and we all watched Andy Andrews' DVD version of *Mastering the Seven Decisions that Determine Personal Success.*[3]

Over the next 18 months, we experienced a tremendous turnaround in our department. People began to enjoy coming to work, and our staff meetings had high and positive energy. We clapped, we laughed, and we focused on the positive. The change was so significant that we were recognized by our hospital's president. She even came and attended one of our staff meetings at which we gave her a standing ovation. The most gratifying thing was that we were adding value to the organization. We had meaning and worth, and it was all due to the tremendous work done by our staff.

The greatest lesson I learned from this awakening was that my staff was not the problem. The problem was me, and I didn't even realize it. Years of success had produced a subtle arrogance, causing managerial and leadership blindness. Looking back, I now realize that they were ready and waiting to be led, but they needed a leader. They needed someone who believed in them, someone they could trust, and someone they could respect!

I also learned that tomorrow's success is based on the choices you make today. Even though choices are made in an instant, a lack of commitment to act and follow through causes most people to fail.

The following chapters will take you on a journey of transformation, starting with describing what went wrong and traveling through different elements of my managerial and leadership philosophy. These elements are crucial for transformation to happen in you and your organization. My hope is that, as you read about these elements, you will experience and practice *Transformational Management and Leadership*.

The greatest lesson I learned from this awakening was that my staff was not the problem. The problem was me, and I didn't even realize it.

CHAPTER 2

WHAT WENT WRONG?

What went wrong? Well… there were many things that went wrong, but looking back, I have identified four areas that caused the apathy found in our department: Complacency, Stagnation, Relationships, and Failure. Each of these areas is tied to the others. The first three, if not attended to, will result in the fourth: Failure.

COMPLACENCY – THE ARROGANCE OF SUCCESS

Earlier, I alluded to the subtle arrogance that I had developed over the years, which was based on my previous success as a manager. Early on in my career, I attended all of the seminars I could on topics related to management and leadership. I had a desire to learn and apply what I had learned. I was eager and had a lot of energy, and I worked on developing relationships with everyone I met.

At that time, *networking* was the new buzz word, and I excelled at it. I found myself enjoying the experience of developing new relationships and nurturing those relationships, not only with staff but also throughout the whole organization. I knew that my success was tied to developing mutually-beneficial relationships with people in other departments.

Over the years, I cultivated a reputation for being someone who people could come to in order to get something done. I seemed to always get things done and was excelling. As the years passed by, instead of seeking advice from experienced managers and leaders whom I trusted, I found that I was the one people were coming to for advice. Somewhere along the way, I had crossed that line from newbie to a trusted resource and veteran. I was honest, trustworthy, loyal, and a team player. I was satisfied, happy, and rested on my laurels. In other words, I had become complacent.

Ironically, it was over those same years that I started to lose the energy and desire to excel. Networking had become a passing thought, mainly because I had come to know a tremendous amount of people. This is both a blessing and curse of longevity in an organization.

I had seen the consultants come and go, trumpeting their latest ideas on how to reorganize, streamline, and improve the organization. I also found myself becoming cynical about each new initiative being pushed. Negativity and cynicism became an ever-growing presence in my world. Outwardly, I was still the friendly and outgoing person everyone knew me to be, but little did they know of the battles being waged inside of me.

I was losing ground and found myself hating my job and dreading going to work. What was once second-nature had become drudgery. This feeling brought with it an attitude of smothering perfectionism. I passed this attitude along to my staff in the way of unfair expectations. I was surviving, but I had become complacent to the point of stagnation.

Inwardly, I had become and represented everything that I despised in a manager and leader. In my department, the environment was becoming a pressure cooker, and I was the stove providing the heat.

STAGNATION – THE ENEMY OF EXCELLENCE

I sincerely believe that stagnation is the brother of complacency. There is a fine line between being content with what one has accomplished and resting on those accomplishments. If you're not aware of your current state, you will soon find that you are not growing or learning any longer, making you vulnerable to stagnation.

It is an insidious process that can only occur through vanity, arrogance, and a big ego. Ironically, I did not think of myself as having any of those three characteristics or traits. That is why the revelations I spoke of earlier were so sobering. We will discuss this spiral of doom, "The Destructive Performance Cycle," in another chapter.

> *It is an insidious process, which can only occur through vanity, arrogance, and a big ego.*

The American Heritage Dictionary defines *stagnation* as, "Foul from standing still; polluted; stale." That about sums up the state in which I found myself. I had to chuckle when I read that because I knew I was making a lot of people unhappy. Throw in some personal health issues I was dealing with at the time, and *voilà*, you have the recipe for a living, breathing, moving, and toxic dump of negativity. I just hope and pray I was not as bad as I now perceived myself to be, but that's what happens when you find yourself in a place with seemingly no way out.

If you have ever seen a stagnant pond, you have probably seen the results of a lack of movement. When a pond ceases to have any current or flow to bring in fresh water, it becomes stale, foul-smelling, and polluted. Pretty soon, the birds and wildlife quit using it as a place of replenishment.

The same can be said for leadership. In his book, *The 21 Indispensable Qualities of a Leader: Becoming the Person Others Will Want to Follow*, John C. Maxwell made a great observation about this concept as it pertains to leaders. He pointed out the following consequence for leaders: "The day they stop growing is the day they forfeit their potential – and the potential of the organization."[1] And that was precisely what I realized was my problem. I had no current or flow and was not replenishing my role as leader. I had quit growing, learning, and challenging myself. I had lost faith in those I had hired, and I was on the verge of losing faith in myself.

But with a stagnant pond, as you restore the flow of water and get it moving again, the birds and wildlife return. There is a new excitement, and life begins to flourish and grow again. Throw in some sunlight, and you are off to the races.

The same could be said for your leadership. I have learned and now understand that life occurs in cycles. I have identified certain cycles we move through during our lives and careers. They will be discussed in detail as we move along our journey toward *Transformational Management and Leadership.*

RELATIONSHIPS – SUCCESS NEGATED

Relationships are the keys to your success. Come on and repeat after me: "Relationships are the keys to MY success." Again, but this time, louder and with a lot more energy! "RELATIONSHIPS ARE THE KEY TO MY SUCCESS!" Without relationships, there is no success, no fulfillment, no sense of accomplishment, no worth, and certainly no sense of teamwork.

It takes people to get things done. It takes people to make up a team, and it takes positive relationships with the team members for the team to perform effectively. This means that because you are managing and leading people, you need to be a people person—if you want to be successful, that is.

Sure, people will do what you say because you have the authority to make them do it. While relying on this form of authority may bring some short-term success, it will result in long-term failure. It will also result in **high** turnover rates, **low** quality, **low** performance, **low** output, and **low** morale.

If you lead like this—and believe me, many do—you will find yourself facing failure in possibly every aspect of your life. Why would I make such a claim? Because life is based on relationships, and I do not believe you can treat people one way at work, and then flip the switch to treat others outside of work as if work never happened. If you can, you're one of the few. Personally, I have never met anyone who could accomplish this.

In our department, I had a staff that was very experienced. We had a low turnover rate, and I had managed them for many years. Over the years, I must have been doing something right; or, was I? What I came to realize was that I had forgotten the basic premise of maintaining positive relationships with each one of our employees. I came to view everything they did in a negative light, and I forgot about all of the positives they brought to the table.

> *What chance of success do you really think you are going to have if you view your staff in such a negative light?*

I didn't recognize when they did something right. Instead, I engaged them on every action in which they did not perform up to my standards. Compliments were scarce, but tension was not. Remember, I was the stove that brought the heat to the pressure cooker. What chance of success did I really have as a manager if I viewed my staff in such a negative light? I'll ask you the same question. What chance of success do you really think you are going to have if you view your staff in such a negative light?

The questions you should be asking are what John G. Miller asked in his book, *QBQ! The Question Behind the Question*. I highly recommend you read this book. He asked, "What can I do to make a difference?" and "How can I support the team?"[2] The latter is the tougher question which most people's egos will not allow them to ask themselves.

I now realized that, in order for me to be successful, I had to re-establish positive relationships with my staff. I also needed to change my perspective and attitude toward their performance. Would it be easy? No. Would it be difficult? You bet!

You see, you just can't change overnight. If the staff senses you are insincere about what you are doing, then all is lost, and they'll chalk it up to just another gimmick. If this happens, then what follows is more of the same troubles that brought you to this point to begin with; this time, it will be worse. Why worse? You have just compounded the problems, and it will be harder to regain their trust and respect. As one employee told his manager, "You don't understand. We hate you! You'll have to work your way up to mistrust."

So... why not commit to changing **YOUR** *perspective,* **YOUR** *attitude,* and **YOUR** *performance*! You may find out, like me, that you have a staff eager and willing to be led, but they just need a leader. How about challenging yourself to become a force of positive energy, and change how you relate to your employees?

> *Be a leader, one that inspires and one that your staff can have confidence in, respect, and follow not because they have to but because they want to!*

If you believe that you are such a good manager and leader, how about stepping back to take a look at yourself, take an inventory of the positives you bring to the table, and share that with your staff in a positive manner? Be a leader, one that inspires and one that your staff can have confidence in, respect, and follow not because they have to but because they want to!

This is where the transformation begins. It begins with **you**—not your staff! In my case, it began with **ME!**

FAILURE – VULNERABILITY UNMASKED

Have you ever sat back and thought about what failure means to you? In the past, I never did. I have now come to believe that one cannot have success without failure.

As I look back over the years of my career, I still do not see where I really had any failures. Maybe, I didn't frame my setbacks as failures? I really don't remember. As I was growing up poor and working my way through college, failure simply was not an option. It was a luxury I could not afford.

Let's take a look at failure, what it means, and why we see it the way we do. When faced with losing control of the department and sensing my failure as a manager and leader, I did not handle it very well. Now that I am on the other side of the transformation, my perspective has changed in how I view failure.

Failure can be described as "one's inability to meet an objective or task." In the simplest of terms, that is true. With failure, comes pressure. Pressure can occur when one starts to think about failing. If you put these two together, before you know it, you can become a victim of your own thinking.

Pressure can lead one to make bad choices, and it is here where people fail. Thoughts can and will influence actions. Failure is the result of bad choices.

In his book, *Mastering the Seven Decisions that Determine Personal Success,* Andy Andrews does a tremendous job of explaining the power of our choices. According to Mr. Andrews, we are the sum total of our collective decisions. In other words, you are where you are today as a result of the collective decisions you have made from the time you were born.

Take this book for example. You made the decision to read it. I believe that was a good choice. Now, this is where it gets good, and this is where it hit home with me. Mr. Andrews goes on to state that if we are the sum total of our decisions, you therefore can make different decisions and put yourself in a different place. In other words, if you make better decisions, your situations will turn out better. I know it sounds like stating the obvious, but how many people do you know who continue to make bad decisions that continue to lead to bad outcomes? Why is that?

As in QBQ, the lesson learned here is that the situations in which we find ourselves are based on our decisions, both good and bad. Want to change your circumstances? Make better decisions. You're in control of that process. It is a choice, and how you decide to respond to your situations will determine your outcomes.

> *The lesson learned here is that the situations in which we find ourselves are based on our decisions, both good and bad.*

As I stated earlier, this is why my revelations were so freeing. I found that I was actually in control of my own destiny. No one else but me! I was not a victim. This feeling was so empowering and exhilarating that it's hard to describe. I rediscovered an energy that I had not felt in a long, long time. I had a purpose and could sense a confidence within myself that seemed lost long ago. I felt like "Maverick" in the movie, *Top Gun*, having re-engaged the enemy, but this time, I would be armed with different ammunition.

It has been said that success is simply the end result of many failures strung together. That may be true, but others believe that success is not merely the end result of a process; it's what you become along the way. Either way, I was now engaged in that process.

Once you frame your journey this way, you start to change **YOUR** perspective, **YOUR** attitude, and **YOUR** performance. This is the essence of the transformation we'll be discussing. This brings us to what I consider to be the heart of this book. How do I get from the state I am currently in to the transformation I so desperately want? The rest of the book will help you to lay the foundation for that transformation, culminating with a guide to putting it all together.

CHAPTER 3

TRANSFORMATIONAL MANAGEMENT

You have been reading about my struggles; now, I'm going to talk about how I transformed those struggles into success.

The word, *transform*, is defined as, "to change markedly the form or appearance of."[1] This brings us to the question of what is "Transformational Management?" It is a philosophy of management that focuses on the personal growth of the leader and is applied through the development of positive relationships.

The philosophy is based on a process that changes Perspectives, Attitudes, and Performance through *transforming* yourself, your staff, and your environment. It uses the 5 C's of Leadership to change a culture. It embraces a "Valued Team Member Philosophy" to uplift and inspire your staff while improving quality and service. Transformational Management focuses on 3 areas:

- Personal growth and development
- Relationships
- Employee/staff development

It utilizes what I call, "relational management," to connect you with your staff. The uniting of these two forces, management and staff, is what produces tremendous success. It is based on the premise that your staff is a direct reflection of your managerial and leadership style. In other words, they won't change or grow until you change and grow. You must be transformed to help lead others to their own transformation.

The bad news is that it depends on you. The good news is that it depends on you! You control how much of a transformation takes place in you, your employees, and in your workplace environment.

You may have concerns about those you answer to, whether to a boss or to a board. You are concerned that this type of approach will not work because those you answer to are hard to deal with and have unrealistic expectations. This is not the case. You can only control what you can control, but you can influence beyond your control through your relationships with those to whom you answer. It may take some time, especially with those who are hard to deal with, but it will work.

People that are hard to deal with want one thing and one thing only: results! They want results so they will look good, and when they see you changing your department or organization for the better, they'll want to know what is going on. To change their perspective, you will need to be consistent. This will lead them to a change of attitude towards you and those you lead. They will start to support you more as things change for the better.

It will take different timeframes for different personality types to change, some sooner and some later. Some will never change. I believe this will be self-evident. If this is the case, I would suggest that you look for another place to lead or someone else worthy of your trust and talent.

I have come to learn that leadership is not about control or authority; it is about influence. Once you change, you will automatically change the dynamics of your relationship with, not only your staff, but also with those to whom you answer. This is where your influence starts.

The same could be said for your staff. Some will come on board quickly, and some never will. Have confidence that the majority of your staff will embrace the new you! A small minority will never embrace you no matter what you do. These are the low performers who delight in negativity, keep the pot stirred, and sit back in a state of blissful ignorance. They are satisfied by a warped sense of self-gratification and accomplishment as seen on modern-day reality TV shows. Only now, it is affecting your workplace environment. These are your know-it-alls who I classify as cynics. My advice to you is to move these people out ASAP! They are a cancer that can't be tolerated. Be forewarned, if you have a human resource department, be ready to do battle in a legal sense.

> *Have confidence that the majority of your staff will embrace the new you!*

In the end, results drive your decisions, but legalism drives your human resource department. You care about performance and results; they care about performance and documentation. You are responsible for getting things done. They are responsible for not getting sued.

I am not saying they are bad; believe me, I'm not. I have friends and colleagues who work in human resources. By and large, they do the best job they can under difficult circumstances, but they cannot do it alone. They need your help with consistent and accurate documentation.

I was fortunate enough to work with a wonderful HR representative, Karen Regan. We got off to a bit of a rocky start due to our lack of necessary documentation to do what needed to be done. To be honest, it was abysmal. We immediately put in place new documentation standards. By working together through the issues, we developed great documentation and a relationship built on trust and respect.

To help you with this process, Transformational Management implements "On-time Coaching" as part of its valued team member philosophy. Documented "On-time Coaching" sessions improve documentation to assist in moving low performers out when needed. As part of "Performance-based Coaching," they help to improve and maximize the performance of your middle and high performers. This is done by consistent and timely feedback regarding performance.

Once you move the low performers out, take the opportunity to change your environment with the people you hire. Hire for attitude, and teach skill. Sure, people have to have the aptitude to do the job. Though, you should hire employees that have good attitudes. I have found that sometimes the most senior people or those with the most experience cause the most trouble. That is why, in nursing, I was not afraid to hire new graduates with good attitudes. They brought a positive attitude to the team and a willingness to learn and grow that some experienced personnel had lost.

Granted, I am brushing with a broad stroke, but I do not believe experience necessarily trumps attitude. A good attitude with good experience is the ideal. A good rule of thumb from my point of view is to hire for attitude and teach skill. This will be discussed in detail later in the book.

RELATIONAL MANAGEMENT DEFINED

What is *Relational Management*? Let us first look at the words that make up the definition: relation and management. *Relation* is defined as "an existing connection; a significant association between or among things; the relation between cause and effect."[2] *Management* is defined as "the person or persons controlling and directing the affairs of a business, institution, etc." and is distinguished from *labor*.[3]

I define Relational Management as developing a significant relationship or connection with each employee so there can be a positive cause-and-effect between management and staff. It is employee-focused and quality-driven. This significant relationship or connection is at the crux of success for both the employee and the manager. Why is this so important? This one relationship drives all facets of service: the work environment/culture, quality, morale, and customer satisfaction.

> *This significant relationship or connection is at the crux of success for both the employee and the manager.*

You may ask, how do I make this connection? Get to know your employees. This may sound simple and obvious, but you would be amazed by how many managers do not know their employees.

I will give you an example. My wife works where I had worked, and we had been married for seven years before her manager at the time realized we were married. I am convinced that the only reason he put it together was because he came into my office one day when my wife was visiting, wondering why she was there.

You make the connection with your employees by visiting with them. This provides them with encouragement. Mark Sanborn captures this in his book *The Encore Effect*, which is about achieving remarkable performances. He said,

> Encouragement is the grease that allows the wheels of inspiration and instruction to turn efficiently. Think about how you respond to encouragement. Those around you need it in the same way.[4]

He goes on to explain that you have to establish a positive relationship before you can start giving feedback. Otherwise, it will not be accepted as intended and will be looked upon as criticism. Andy Andrews explains it this way:

> Leadership essentially boils down to two things: your perspective or belief about yourself, and a quality we can call 'likeability.' Likeability can be defined as the ability to build rapport so that others will listen to you. We listen to the people we like.[5]

Without making this crucial connection with those you lead, you can't influence. Thus, you won't be able to lead, at least, not effectively. This is where I see most leaders fail. They see leadership through the lens of authority and control—not influence. They sacrifice long-term success for short-term gain.

While visiting, find out what your employees' stories are and how they came to work for you. When I took over managing a 32-bed Medical Intensive Care Unit, I inherited 120 employees. On average, 20-24 employees would be there for 12-hour shifts for both days and nights. Initially, I would visit with each employee every day. If the unit was busy, I would sometimes visit twice per day.

> *It all starts with developing positive relationships, the critical connection between you and those you lead.*

Twice a week, I would visit with the night crew. I came in early to see them prior to their leaving, or I would stay late to see them start their shift. Occasionally, I would show up unannounced to visit with them during their shift. This meant I was visiting a max of 24-48 times daily.

Was I perfect in doing this every day? No, but the point is that you should set aside some time each day or week to visit with your employees. Some may consider this to be going overboard, but this is exactly what your staff needs. It all starts with developing positive relationships, the critical connection between you and those you lead.

I would advise erring on the side of visiting too much rather than too little, especially in the initial phase. I did it frequently in the beginning until the staff got used to seeing me, and then I settled into a regular routine with a goal of visiting once per day for the dayshift staff and twice per week for the nightshift staff. It is important for them to see you out and about, interacting with them. This establishes visibility, accessibility, and immediately starts addressing the three needs of employees in the workplace setting.

SUCCESS UNITED – EMPLOYEES AND MANAGEMENT

How did the staff respond to these visitations? They absolutely loved it! I was careful to visit with each employee. If I missed one, I would circle back around to make sure I talked to that person. While doing this, I got to learn their names, their stories, and what I could do to help them succeed at work. I also learned what they had to overcome in order to do their jobs effectively.

I let them get to know me. I thanked them and told them how glad I was to see them. I let them know how much we needed them,[6] and I reminded them about the difference they were making in our patient's lives. I complimented them on things I observed them doing well. I also used this time to tell them what we were doing to improve the workplace environment. I used what John Maxwell calls the "30-second rule,"[7] which is the practice of saying something encouraging or positive to the employee within the first 30 seconds of your conversation. It is a powerful tool, and you can read more about it and other techniques for building positive relationships with people in his book, *25 Ways to Win with People: How to Make Others Feel Like a Million Bucks.* I highly recommend this book, and I use his techniques often.

We also celebrated the high performers of the day. We bragged about them in front of the other staff,[8] and we helped them to experience what employees want most out of their work:

- Acknowledgement
- Affirmation
- The opportunity to add value

The first two are part of what is addressed by Maxwell's 30-second rule.[9] Employees want to be acknowledged. This makes them feel valued. When you acknowledge them and their contributions, it gives them a feeling of being valued. Maxwell calls this "adding value" to employees. You can also add value by growing and developing them.

The 30-second rule is one of the most powerful tools you have available in making this connection. Once you make that connection, you're well on your way to changing your staff's perspectives.

They also want *affirmation*. In other words, they want to know that what they are doing has worth and meaning. They do not want their work to be in vain. By acknowledging them and their contributions, you affirm their place within the team.

Last, but not least, they want to *add value*. We must not forget that they, too, want to add value to the organization.

This is done through their performance. The quality of that value depends on how well we develop them!

In order to address these three areas, the first thing you have to do is work on yourself. Establishing these connections takes time, effort, and consistency.

Ask yourself this question: if you are unwilling to invest time in your employees, why would you expect them to invest their time in your department, your vision, and your goals? They will not, and they'll simply be content to pick up a paycheck and nothing more. This connection will not happen overnight, but do not underestimate the practice of visiting with your employees. Without it, you cannot unite staff with management, and without this unity, you'll never set the foundation for the success or transformation you desire.

> *Ask yourself this question: if you are unwilling to invest time in your employees, why would you expect them to invest their time in your department, your vision, and your goals?*

PROS AND CONS

I will not belabor this point because the whole book speaks to the pros of initiating this type of transformation, but I will speak to it briefly. The biggest pro is it will transform every aspect of your life, thus transforming everyone who relates or interacts with you. This includes those you manage, lead, and do business with.

It is based on continual learning which I have learned can be equated to continual renewal. You will see a return of that desire, energy, and positive attitude many of you experienced leaders had early on in your careers. Newer managers and leaders will also experience a renewed energy. This is because both groups (experienced and new) will now have the answer they have been looking for and the control over how to respond. This will bring with it a commitment to action that will be the fuel to start moving that heavy wheel of apathy toward a transformed and engaged work environment.

> *By transforming yourself, you will learn new skills and re-establish a long-lost confidence, enabling you to confront the challenges to come.*

Transforming a culture or environment is a tough job that many are not equipped to handle. By transforming yourself, you will learn new skills and re-establish a long-lost confidence, enabling you to confront the challenges to come.

Is it the be-all and end-all for all of your leadership challenges? No. For one to find true happiness and peace, one cannot discount the spiritual side of our existence. For me, that has been my Christian faith. The revelations and awakenings described herein reconnected those two facets: my work life and my personal life.

I really do not see any cons with this philosophy. I would caution you to keep in mind that, as your energy increases and you begin engaging your staff, it will take energy to keep up the work needed to make the transformation. Once relationships have been established or re-established, they need to be maintained. This takes energy and awareness and is an area where many fall short. A crucial element to maintaining proper energy levels is to take the appropriate time to recharge your batteries, so to speak, both mentally and physically. In other words, be careful not to grind beyond your limits.

Athletes refer to this as getting into negative returns. Driven individuals really have to be careful here and can be caught off-guard, drained of all energy, and left wondering what happened. They are surprised because what others see as a grind, they see as fulfilling work.

The message here is to take care of yourself both mentally and physically. This will help you to keep your energy supply built up so that you can maintain the momentum you'll be creating.

Now that we have introduced the concept of "Transformational Management," we will turn our attention to the "Leadership" part of the equation. We will explore the processes and steps needed to make the transformation a reality. It does, indeed, take leadership. As John Maxwell often states, the first person you need to learn how to lead is yourself! This is what I had forgotten and had to rediscover.

CHAPTER 4

THE 5 C'S OF LEADERSHIP

The Five C's of Leadership are the core principles that will enable you to lead effectively. The principles begin with commitment and end with consistency. They are interrelated and build upon each other. When applied together, they will become your cornerstone to success. Collectively, they represent the essence and substance of leadership. The Five C's provide the foundation upon which you can build your leadership. They generate integrity instead of manipulation, substance instead of symbolism. These principles will help you to begin influencing, which is the definition of leadership.

It used to be said that management was separated out from leadership, but I am one who has never bought into that line of thought. Management was always characterized as being task-oriented, dealing with day-to-day duties and operations. Leadership was characterized as providing the vision, inspiring the people, and motivating people to do things they ordinarily wouldn't do.

In the end, managers have to lead, and leaders have to manage. Whether it's day-to-day organizational tasks or implementing organizational vision, leaders and managers have to do both.

Take a look around you today, not only in the workplace, but out in the community. Do you see many leaders?

We have a serious lack of leadership in our society. Take one look at Washington, and if that does not convince you, I don't know what will.

You and your staff will collectively shape the environment and culture of your department and organization at large. The resulting culture or environment directly reflects your leadership. You will have to provide the leadership to implement your own vision or whatever vision you are responsible for implementing.

Before we dive into talking about the Five C's, there is one critical leadership quality that I believe all leadership must be built upon: *integrity*. The Five C's cannot exist without it. As my mom used to tell me about politicians, "If they're not crooked when they go in, they're crooked when they come out." Now, that's a cynical view, but how many of you were shaking your head in agreement when you read that statement?

One night, I was watching an interview with John Huntsman about his book, *Winners Never Cheat: Even in Difficult Times*. He is one of the richest men in the world. Before his chemical company went public, it was the largest family-owned business in the world, with a net worth of over 12 billion dollars. He also founded the Huntsman Cancer Institute, and he stated that after he dies, his fortune will be given away.

In the interview, he was talking about leadership and integrity. He attributed a quote to Sir Winston Churchill about integrity. It struck a nerve with me, so I grabbed a legal pad and wrote it down. He said Churchill stated, "With integrity, nothing else counts. Without integrity, nothing else counts."

I also learned that John Huntsman was the only member of President Richard Nixon's staff not to be called to testify before Congress during the Watergate hearings. It was largely due to his reputation of integrity. After listening to him for one minute, you would understand why. He is truly an American treasure, hero, and patriot.

I believe integrity is the foundation upon which all leadership is built. Noted author on leadership, Ken Blanchard, states that it is the number one attribute employees look for in a leader. You cannot lead if you do not have it. It is that simple. A leader without integrity will eventually be exposed as a fraud like a drunk stopped for DUI trying to explain that he was only drinking water while holding a beer.

> *I believe integrity is the foundation upon which all leadership is built.*

Having discussed the importance of integrity, let us now turn our attention to the Five C's of leadership:

- Commitment
- Concern
- Confidence
- Communication
- Consistency

COMMITMENT

To change a culture, an attitude, or an environment, one must have a vision, a belief in that vision, and a commitment to act upon that belief. Only through a sincerity of change that comes from within will a true commitment to that action produce the desired change. Without this sincerity of commitment, your staff will notice the insincerity, and you will damage whatever credibility you have with them. You could call it a genuineness of action.

Without commitment, change will not occur. Without sincerity, there is no commitment. One cannot exist without the other. Your staff will notice your level of sincerity before anything else, and this is what they will use to gauge your level of commitment. Again, they will believe what they perceive, and they will always believe what they see!

Commitment comes directly from your convictions. Actions speak to your intent. Words mean things, but as the old saying goes, actions speak louder than words. Remember, they will always believe what they see, but they won't always believe what you say. Decisions without action are merely thoughts. This occurs every day with leaders. This is paralysis by analysis: "Yeah, I am going to do this, and I am going to do that, but first…" Then, nothing else follows. This breeds nothing but frustration and confusion with the people you lead. It also leads to low morale and low quality of product.

When employees are watching what you are doing, they're actually trying to determine your intent and level of commitment based on your actions. In other words, they will judge just how much you believe in what you are doing based on what you say you are going to do, when you do it, and how you do it. This is why communication is so important and why your words should match your actions.

Commitment is also key to implementing your vision. If you think of your vision as a car, commitment is the engine that will power your car (vision). The type of transmission (team) you build and place in the car (vision) will determine its speed and performance.

Communication is the fuel for that engine (commitment). The type of fuel (communication) you use will determine what type of mileage you get out of your car (vision) and whether it sputters or accelerates. Think of positive communication as premium-grade fuel and negative communication as diesel. Diesel is the fuel that produces all of the black smoke and blacks up the backend of one's car. If you use diesel fuel in a gas engine, you will experience major problems, including shutdown of the car. The same can occur with your vision.

What is lacking in this illustration is a key piece of equipment. Did you notice? If you said, "key," you are the high performer of the moment! The car cannot run without the key igniting the engine. The key is *action*. All of this is for naught if you are not committed to taking action.

Beliefs drive convictions, and convictions drive commitment. Think of it this way. The strength of your beliefs is expressed through your convictions. This is demonstrated to those you lead through your actions, which tell them of your desire.

How much are you willing to sacrifice in order to make the transformation/vision come to fruition? How willing are you to engage and work with staff to develop an environment for them to succeed through relationships, structures, and resources? Once those you lead gauge your level of desire and commitment, they will either start to believe or to doubt your commitment to improving the workplace environment.

> *Once those you lead gauge your level of desire and commitment, they will either start to believe or to doubt your commitment to improving the workplace environment.*

All of the Five C's of Leadership are linked together and build upon each other. It is our responsibility to make sure we link them.

To me, commitment is everything. You're either all-in or all-out. You will get what you accept and tolerate. What do I mean by this? If you are routinely lax, don't pay attention to detail, and do not follow up or communicate effectively, those you lead will demonstrate those same characteristics. Why? Because they have determined that if it is acceptable to you to lead that way, it must be acceptable for them to perform that way.

CONCERN

At the heart of transformational management and leadership is changing one's heart and perspective, not only in how one thinks but in how one acts. Your actions will reveal your true concerns to those you lead. Andy Stanley captures this so eloquently when he points out,

> The unresolved issues stirring around undetected in your heart will eventually work their way to the surface. Specifically, they'll seep into your actions, your character, and your relationships.[1]

People need to feel valued, not only as employees, but as human beings. They need to have a feeling of self-worth. They need to feel that they are a part of something important. This gives them meaning. The only way to fulfill this need for self-worth, meaning, and inclusion is through concern.

> *People need to feel valued, not only as employees, but as human beings. They need to have a feeling of self-worth.*

They also need to feel good about what they are doing. By showing your concern for them, you create a sense of belonging, meaning, and fulfillment. It makes them feel necessary to your operations. Everyone, regardless of what they might say, longs for this type of significance.

You are reading this book because you long to make a difference and to become significant. It's human nature. President Reagan said, "Never take a man's hope away; it may be all he has." Have you ever seen someone without hope? I have. Our country is full of those who have lost all hope. Have you ever seen how someone responds when shown just a little attention by way of a compliment or by simply acknowledging him or her with a simple "hello?"

I made it a habit to make eye contact with as many people as possible as I walked around at work, saying a friendly "hello" as we passed. One day, this lady who worked in our material services department approached me and told me how much she appreciated that I acknowledged her. She said, "I know you don't know who I am, but I really appreciate you saying 'hey' to me whenever you see me." We went on to have a nice conversation. My acknowledgment gave her a feeling of self-worth, which made her feel good and included in the organization.

Employees also need to know that their leaders are concerned about them and are interested in their well-being. This became crystal clear to me when one of my employees gave some feedback to me during a difficult time in her life. This particular employee's father had died. I had called her several times without successfully making contact with her. I finally left a message on her answering machine. I followed that up with a sympathy card. After returning to work, she stopped me in the unit while I was out visiting with staff. As she thanked me for recognizing her father's death, her eyes began to tear up. She told me that she had never had a manager do anything like that for her. I walked away stunned by this sad commentary, but I am glad that I took the time to recognize something that was so important to one of my employees.

I have found that when employees know that you care and are concerned about their well-being, they'll become concerned about helping you succeed through improved performance. As they realize that they are important to you, you'll start to become important to them.

When concern is present in your organization, you'll start noticing employees going out of their way to help out. Some refer to this as "going the extra mile." Concern helps to bond the relationships with those you lead, which enhances the quality of your workplace environment.

How do you show your employees that you are concerned about them? The first step is to listen to them, not just listening to a few of them, but listening to each one. Don't just listen to the most verbose or popular ones. Pay attention to each person. Take time out to get to know them. Again, meet with them, and ask them to tell you their stories. Not only did I find this interesting, it also gave me an insight into what made them tick. Just by building a solid relationship with your people, you will do what most managers do not. I refer to this type of listening as active listening.

How many of you have seen leaders messing with their phones, texting, and reading e-mails at different times during meetings? Are they listening? Are they engaged? They may be hearing and multi-tasking, but they are not listening or engaged. There is a difference between hearing and listening. I find this practice disrespectful to all in attendance, especially to your employees. Believe me, your employees notice the disrespectful nature of this practice and talk about it amongst themselves after such meetings. This damages your credibility and conveys a lack of sincerity to those you lead.

> *Take time out to get to know them. Again, meet with them, and ask them to tell you their stories.*

Set aside time each day or week to listen to and talk with your employees. While doing so, you will make them feel great about themselves and about what they are doing. Recognize their birthdays, celebrate their successes, offer support and condolences if they lose a loved one, and send them well-wishes if they are ill.

This is not rocket science, but what it does require is that you take time out of your busy schedule to do it. Make it a priority, and do not allow yourself any excuses. Remember to do this especially with those you do not like but are responsible for.

I had a colleague I did not quite mesh with. In fact, I tried to avoid this individual as much as I could. The problem was that I couldn't do my job without interacting with this person. We played phone tag and basically e-mailed back and forth. One day, I decided that I would take a chance and e-mail this person during a time I knew she would be in her office. I replied to one of her e-mails, and at the end of it, I said, "If I haven't told you lately, I appreciate all that you have done to help me." I actually sat there for what seemed like 10 minutes, hesitating to hit the send button.

I sent it, and within one minute, my phone rang, and it was you-know-who on the other end. We had a great conversation, and it changed our whole relationship. This individual even came to my office the next day, and we talked for an hour. I mainly listened, but it gave me a whole new appreciation for her and the job that she was doing. Those were the best 16 words I have ever sent over e-mail.

Many are uncomfortable showing concern for their employees. They either feel too awkward or are too insecure to show such sincerity. I do not know the reason behind this, but I see it all too often. Maybe they think it is a sign of weakness, don't care, or they are just socially insecure. What I do know is if your employees sense that you are sincere, they'll see through the awkwardness and insecurity, and they will appreciate your attempts. It will make you a winner with your staff, and their respect for you will grow dramatically. I am amazed at how much a little interest will elevate people's morale.

Make a difference, and show sincere interest in those you lead. When you are comfortable with showing a little interest, start showing a lot of it! You will be uplifted and inspired by their response.

CONFIDENCE

Confidence is critical to the success of any leader. It provides an essential cohesiveness to the Five C's of Leadership.

> *Confidence should represent self-assuredness concerning one's capabilities but not to the point of arrogance.*

Confidence should represent a self-assuredness concerning one's capabilities but not to the point of arrogance. No one likes an arrogant leader. I know I don't. But people respect a confident one. They also respect one that shows humility. A truly confident person, in this sense, has no trouble showing humility. They have the confidence to admit when they are wrong.

Insecurity breeds arrogance. Insecure people are continually trying to reaffirm and bolster their confidence. They do this by over-compensating with what they say and do, never admitting their errors because of their insecurity. This constant process ends up fortifying the insecurity that they are striving to overcome.

Confidence does many things in regard to management and staff relations. On my first day as the interim manager of our Medical Surgical Intensive Care Unit, I was out and about, making rounds and visiting with the staff. I immediately started the process of getting to know them. I wanted to portray to them that I was not going to be one that sat in the office, barked out orders, and remained unengaged. I wanted to put their minds at ease, knowing I was confident enough to come out to meet and engage them in their environment. By doing so, I got to know them and listened to their concerns. I started making that connection as quickly as I could.

Each day, I walked through the units, visiting with each staff member. I made sure to make eye contact with them. I would spontaneously stop to speak and compliment them as I saw them doing things well. I thanked them for their service and let them know that we would make this a great place to work. I also let them know that we needed their help. I smiled, high-fived them, bragged on them in front of others, and even gave a little knuckle bump every now and then. By doing so, I instilled confidence in them that we were going to do good things. Notice I used the word, "WE." I immediately incorporated them into the equation and made them a part of the team.

In fact, we implemented what I call a "Valued Team Member" philosophy. This also showed them that I was confident enough in my abilities to include them in the process, which was important when it came to changing their perspectives and earning their trust.

Prior to my first day on the job, I had met with the leadership team and gone through a similar process. In that meeting, I listened to their concerns, their goals, their visions, and last but not least, their expectations of me. I told them how honored I was to be a part of the leadership team and that I wanted to show them a different way of managing. I then laid out my philosophy of managing and my vision for the department. We reviewed an action plan I had put together prior to the meeting and later incorporated their ideas into it. At that point, it became OUR vision.

At the end of the presentation, I told them that the only thing I would ask of them was for them to give 100 percent effort toward my vision for the department. I also said that if at the end of my interim role, they did not agree with it, they could ditch it! I asked each one individually to commit to the process in front of the whole team which they did. This meeting took approximately 2 hours. The reason I took this long was that I wanted them to understand where I was coming from and to instill in them a confidence in me that WE as a leadership team were going to do great things. I wanted to maintain and build upon the gains of the previous manager, Andrew Schwier, for whom I have a great deal of respect.

In their book, *The Truth about Leadership: The No-fads, Heart-of-the-Matter Facts You Need to Know,* James M. Kouzes and Barry Z. Posner distinguish "Leadership Competence" from "Technical Competence." Leadership Competence is your ability to mobilize your team in order to get things done while Technical Competence is being skilled or technically proficient.[2]

Do you want to know the results of all of this? In three months, we took a struggling and underperforming unit and started reshaping its culture. We improved morale and put in place structures to help change and improve performance. I can't say enough about how proud I was of the leadership team and the MSICU staff. They got it. As a result, I returned to take the job full-time. The bottom line is that we improved patient care and outcomes that continue until this day.

> *Who would follow a leader who is timid, insecure, and unable to make a decision? Would you?*

By building and improving on the gains of the past, we transformed a culture and unit. In doing so, we turned it into an award-winning unit, receiving quality awards that recognized the staff's excellence in patient care for ventilator-associated pneumonia and central line-associated blood stream infections.

Confidence has many tangible and intangible benefits. A staff needs a confident leader, and they need to be confident in that leader. Who would follow a leader who is timid, insecure, and unable to make a decision? Would you? By the same token, who would follow a leader who is too confident in his or her ability to the point of arrogance, unable to be told anything? I know I wouldn't. If you are not confident in yourself or your abilities, do not expect your staff to be confident in you, follow you, or respect you.

There is an old adage, "If you lack confidence, fake it until you get it!" Be confident, be humble, be positive, and never be afraid to include your staff and leadership team in the decisions that affect them. By doing so, you'll not only gain their trust, you'll gain their confidence. This is where you start building momentum.

COMMUNICATION

Communication is tremendously important to your success. When working with different levels of leadership, this is the one area where I constantly see failure. To this day, I am still a work-in-progress. As described earlier, communication is the fuel that powers the car. Positive or negative communication is crucial. It is

> *Your employees interact with you according to your communication style. The quality of those relationships is based solely on the quality of your communication with them.*

so crucial that even no communication can be seen as negative.

Communication sets the tone with employee relationships. Your employees interact with you through your communication style. The quality of those relationships is based solely on the quality of your communication with them. This is why it is important for you to determine how to communicate with your employees both individually and as a group.

This encompasses everything from the mode of communication to the time of day you communicate with them. This can easily be assessed when you are visiting with your employees. In fact, this facet of leadership will determine your success or failure as a leader.

I had a colleague at work whose manager came into his work area with another manager one day. They were looking for a specific individual. My colleague's manager looked around and then commented to the other manager, "Nobody's here." All of the staff in the room heard this. The other manager, realizing his colleague's gaff, tried to smooth things over, but the damage was already done. My colleague was outraged at being labeled a "nobody" by his manager. He has not forgotten it to this day. The saddest part was that the offending manager never apologized, opting for ego over humility. What do you think this manager's chance for success will be with the staff he offended?

Communication can be separated into 5 categories:

- Honest
- Timely
- Clear
- Positive
- Open

Honest Communication

There is nothing more important in terms of setting the tone with your employees than honest communication. If an employee has no trust in what you are saying, you have no relationship. Through honest communication, you build credibility with your staff.

Forget the politically correct dogma that permeates our society today. Do not filibuster answers to the point that employees will not understand what you are saying. Speak honestly, directly, and sincerely about their concerns. You will gain both their trust and respect.

It's not hard. Be honest with them. You would be amazed by how many leaders try to say something without really saying something. The amazing thing is we're not even talking about politicians! And, God forbid if someone tries to hold them accountable for what they said. Why say it if you are not willing to stand behind it? The answer can be found in one word: manipulation.

> *We live in a society where people do not believe what leaders are saying because the leaders saying it do not believe their own words.*

We live in a society where people do not believe what leaders are saying because the leaders saying it do not believe their own words. They hope that they won't be put on-the-spot or be held to what they said. They say things like, "I'll share the truth with you as I know it to be." What? Since when does the truth need to be qualified? This is indicative of someone who believes in moral relativism. I'll leave that one alone for now, but this is an ever-increasing problem in leadership today. Decide on what you are going to say, and simply say it. Stand by it, and you will see your credibility with your staff soar.

Timely Communication

I cannot express enough or overemphasize the importance of timely communication. This requires diligence and awareness. You may find this to be the most difficult part of communication. The impact of not being timely with your communication can be devastating. Emotions can range from anger to mistrust. It blows your credibility and lowers morale. Nothing good comes from not being timely.

Timeliness also takes planning. Getting information out too quickly to your staff can be equally as devastating as a lack of communication. I would urge you to develop a consistent routine for planning and laying the foundation for how you will communicate with your staff. This is critical when dealing with important pieces of information. It affects their livelihoods, and once you put it out there for everyone to see and hear, you lose all control over how it is used and interpreted.

Through consistency and routine, do your best to help your staff receive information from you. This will help to ward off the rumor mill and will add to your credibility, enhancing your relationship with your staff.

Clear Communication

The ability to communicate clearly affects your ability to implement your goals and vision. Clarity enhances organizational performance. Make it a habit to ensure that your staff understands what you are communicating.

Years ago, when I taught facilitation, we had a saying, "Seek first to understand, then be understood." In this context, you'll be able to gauge your staff's understanding of what you are saying. This will give you the opportunity to clarify. By clarifying, you will have a chance to clear up any misunderstandings. Remember, their reality is what they perceive it to be.

Positive Communication

I could talk all day about this because I believe it is so important. Why? Because it's not the norm. If it was, positive people would not stand out as much as they do. Positive communication is crucial to your success. I do not believe you can have success without it. Whatever success you do have will be shortsighted and short-lived.

Through positive and negative communication, you are shaping your relationships with your staff. Being a positive communicator gives you the ability to uplift and inspire your staff. Leaders are supposed to inspire, are they not? How do they do it? They inspire through positive communication.

This is where motivation takes hold and helps you to build momentum. This is where you start to change your staff's perspective, which leads to changing their attitudes and then their performance. Hmmm... Sound familiar? When this occurs, you change your workplace environment and your organization's culture.

Mike Young, one of our supervisors, would occasionally call me Pollyanna when I first started managing our

Medical Surgical Intensive Care Unit. I accused him of scarring me by calling me such a name, but it did reinforce to me that I was being positive.

Ask yourself this question: "Would you rather work for a leader who is positive or one who is negative?" Be the positive leader that you would want to work for.

Open Communication

Open communication is usually combined with honest communication. I have separated it out because I want to explain what it means to the people you lead. Why is openness so important in communication?

What we're really talking about is transparency. Hidden agendas, secrets, and surprises will damage and crush your credibility when exposed. What is really at stake is your integrity, and we know integrity is everything when it comes to leadership.

Credibility and integrity are character traits that are assigned to us by others based on their perception of what we say and do. We do not have the luxury of assigning those traits to ourselves. If we did, all politicians would be seen as people of credibility and integrity which we know is not the case.

You may be wondering why I mention credibility and integrity separately. Integrity is credibility that has been demonstrated over time. One can be credible from time to time, but to be viewed as a person of integrity, you have to be consistent over time.

The *American Heritage Dictionary* defines *reciprocate* as "moving back and forth from one thing to another; to show or feel in response or return; to interchange or give and take mutually." In the diagram below, you can see how relationships work in what I term the Principle of Reciprocating Relationships:

The Principle of Reciprocating Relationships

Openness $\implies$ Transparency $\implies$ Credibility $\implies$ Integrity

Openness $\impliedby$ Transparency $\impliedby$ Credibility $\impliedby$ Integrity

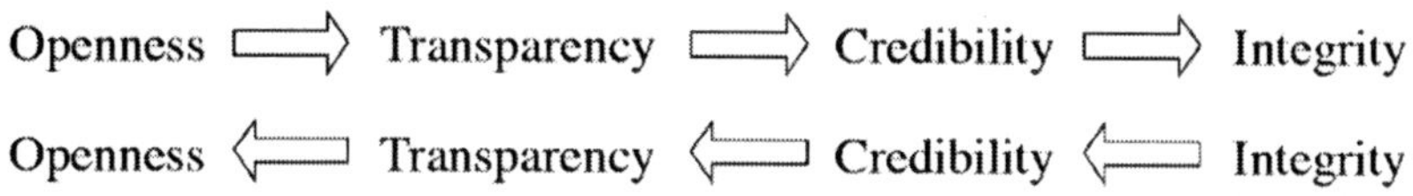

Figure 4.1

As the arrows in the diagram suggest, your credibility increases as you become more open and transparent, which will have a direct effect on your integrity. When consistently applied, people will view you as a person of integrity. This is because you are open and transparent with not only your words but also with your actions.

The reverse is also true as the relationship regressively reciprocates and goes in the opposite direction. When the arrows reverse, the diagram depicts what happens if you start to compromise your integrity, which leads to compromising your credibility. This results in becoming less transparent and less open. This is where hidden agendas and mistrust are birthed. When this occurs, people will view and treat you as a person they cannot trust because you are not open or transparent.

This is a slippery slope that you must avoid at all costs! It takes a long time to build trust, credibility, and integrity, but it only takes seconds to destroy. So, treat it with the respect it deserves, and protect it as the treasure it surely is. Your staff and everyone you interact with will value you all the more.

CONSISTENCY

Consistency plays a key role in one's ability to lead. One cannot be an effective leader without being consistent. Consistency is defined as having "a logical coherence among things or parts."[3] In other words, your words need to match your actions and deeds—and vice versa.

> *When your words and actions consistently match, your staff will start to trust what you are saying and doing.*

Consistency plays such a major role in leadership that people will stay in a bad work environment even if their boss is a terrible boss, as long as he is consistent. In this case, consistency is bad.

Consistency builds the foundation upon which your relationship with staff members will be judged. Your staff will rally around you or desert you based on this one aspect of leadership. How many of you have stated, "I like X, but I wouldn't go into battle with him." What you are alluding to is that he or she is not consistent with his or her behavior. Somewhere along the line, you felt or were actually not supported by the mysterious Mr. or Ms. X.

Consistency, or the lack thereof, either builds trust or mistrust. This depends on how it is or is not applied.

Consistency builds reliability. When your words and actions consistently match, your staff will start to trust what you are saying and doing. They will know how you'll react to different situations. They'll get a sense of your temperament, and this can only be accomplished by being consistent over time. This builds credibility.

When people start to trust and have positive interactions with you, they will start to relax because they will know what to expect from you. This is when performance and morale begins to improve. This improvement will continue but only if their interactions with you are positive.

In *Credibility: How Leaders Gain and Lose It, Why People Demand It*, Kouzes and Posner describe credibility and its impact with employees this way:

> Credible leaders raise self-esteem. Leaders who make a difference to others cause people to feel that they too can make a difference. They set people's spirits free and enable them to become more than they might have thought possible.[4]

What about discipline? How can you be positive when it comes to disciplinary issues? It depends on your organizational culture. Do you have a punitive, disciplinary environment? Or, is it an environment that focuses on performance and how to improve that performance? If you have a good opinion of your staff, you will treat them in a positive manner. If you loathe your staff, you will treat them in a negative manner.

I use the PFP principle: Praise-Feedback-Praise. If it is a situation where no positives can be found, be consistent and fair in your dealings with your staff. The rest of your staff will be watching to see how you handle this challenging situation, so be consistent and fair about it. This will give you credibility with your staff.

A certain percentage of your staff will not adapt or respond to your coaching. As stated earlier, these are your low performers. Give them a chance to rectify their performance, and if they continue to perform below standards and/or are a negative influence within your area of responsibility, move them out as soon as possible. If you cannot move them out, diminish or minimize their effect on your staff, department, or organization. We will discuss this more when we talk about "On-time Coaching."

> *In general, people want to know the type of picture you are painting: your vision, where they fit into that vision, and how you are going to get there.*

Consistency also provides direction for your staff, which helps to transform your workplace environment. In general, people want to know the type of picture you are painting: your vision, where they fit into that vision, and how you are going to get there. Consistency helps you meet those needs.

One thing that will destroy a vision faster than anything is confusion within the workforce due to inconsistency. This could be inconsistency with regard to the vision or to its implementation. Consistency helps your staff focus on the duty at hand. It gets everyone rowing the boat in the same direction, which eventually helps build momentum and confidence in your vision.

Do not underestimate the impact that inconsistency will have on your leadership. You can be committed but still be inconsistent. This lack of consistency will cause those you lead to question your commitment, honesty, sincerity, and other critical aspects of your leadership.

Consistency can be a challenge in the ever-changing environments in which we work. Do not let these changing environments and challenging times cause you to sacrifice your credibility. Rely on consistent communication to keep those you lead informed. By doing so, you will constantly reaffirm your commitment and preserve your credibility.

As we continue on our transformational journey, we'll now explore the key to *Transformational Management and Leadership*. Without it, the transformation cannot take place.

CHAPTER 5

CHANGING PERSPECTIVES, ATTITUDES, AND PERFORMANCE

We have now come to the second part of the book. The first part was simply setting the stage, and the second part will deal with more of the process. I am excited for you. To be honest, I also have some feelings of trepidation. You may ask, "Why the feelings of trepidation?" Well… It's because I know the road that lies ahead, and it must be paved with a brutal honesty that most do not possess. This transformation will be the easiest decision you have ever made, but it will also be the most difficult. Why? I have come to the conclusion that many leaders simply have too big of an ego to take the introspective journey needed to transform the way they think, behave, and perform. If it was simple, everyone would be doing it.

Do not get me wrong. My feelings of trepidation are overwhelmed by the excitement I have for you if you are willing to go down this road. It will be hard work, but it will also be one of the most freeing and liberating experiences you will have. It will free you because the bondage of ego will no longer restrain you. You will learn that there is nothing wrong with a little self-assessment and honesty with one's self. It will also ignite in you a passion to learn and grow. When that switch is flipped on, you're off to the races.

This is when your relationships with those of whom you interact, manage, and lead will change for the better.

Right now, I encourage you to get up and go stand in front of a mirror. Some may think you are crazy, but work with me on this. If you don't have one, then a pocket-sized or desk mirror will do. Look at your reflection in the window if you have to. I want you to close your eyes and concentrate on all of the problems you have been encountering. Take a minute or two to reflect.

After reflecting, I want you to count to ten. When you get to ten, open your eyes and look at the person in the mirror. Take a good, long look. You are now looking at the person who is responsible for the situation you now find yourself in. You can only control what you can control, but by choosing to be a leader, a manager, or a supervisor, you have put yourself in a position of responsibility. Part of that responsibility is to deal with problems caused by either you or by someone else.

I want you to close your eyes again and concentrate on all of the positive qualities you possess as a leader. This is important, so focus on nothing but the positives. Again, take a couple of minutes, then count to ten, and open your eyes. Take another long, hard look at the person in the mirror. You are now looking at the answer to your problems! I know this was a simplistic exercise, but what it did (if you did it right) is show you how easy it is to change your perspective. The hard part comes when you have to apply it.

Anthony Hopkins captures the essence of this dynamic in the movie, *The Edge*.[1] He played the character, Charles Morse. Along with a rival of his played by Alec Baldwin, their plane crashed in the wilderness and they were stalked by a grizzly bear. Charles ultimately became the lone survivor.

In a moment of reflection while answering a reporter's question about his struggle to survive, he stated, "We are all put to the test, but it never comes in the form or the point we would prefer." Ultimately, he and he alone put himself in that position by agreeing to get on the airplane. We do the same by *choosing* to be in leadership.

In leadership, we seldom have the luxury of being able to choose the problems we face. Though, like Charles, we always have a choice of how we respond. As leaders, we need to work on how we respond, and that was the ultimate point of the mirror exercise prescribed earlier. If you change your perspective, you'll change your response.

Your problems are caused, in part, by how you are currently responding to the challenges you face. The solution to those problems can only be discovered through proper responses to those problems. Even though he placed himself in a risky situation, Charles Morse didn't choose to be stalked by a grizzly, but he did show incredible resilience in how he responded to the challenge, which helped him to survive.

This process will require time, consistency of action, and a willingness to stay committed. In short, it's a process—a never-ending, lifelong process. It is also an exciting process that will reshape your destiny and future. The really exciting part is that you are the captain of the ship! You alone are in control of the course you set and the results you get.

Are you at your wits end and looking for answers? Are you experiencing low staff morale, high turnover, and low quality? Is your department or business falling apart, and you're left wondering what went wrong? Then, you are where you need to be in order to make a great transformation. The greater the despair, the greater the transformation.

You are where you are due to the decisions that you have made. That is the hard part to accept. If you accept this, you can also change your situation by making better decisions. Andy Andrews does a tremendous job of explaining this concept. He states,

> *The greater the despair, the greater the transformation.*

> But if you can find the answer to your problems in the mirror—if the solution lies within you—well, there's boundless hope, because you can start working on yourself today.[2]

He refers to this as making the "Responsible Decision," which requires this attitude: "I am responsible for my past and my future."[3] He also explains that "responsibility is about hope and control."[4] When you find that you can determine your own level of success, the chains that bind you to the past will be forever broken.

PERFORMANCE IMPROVEMENT CYCLE

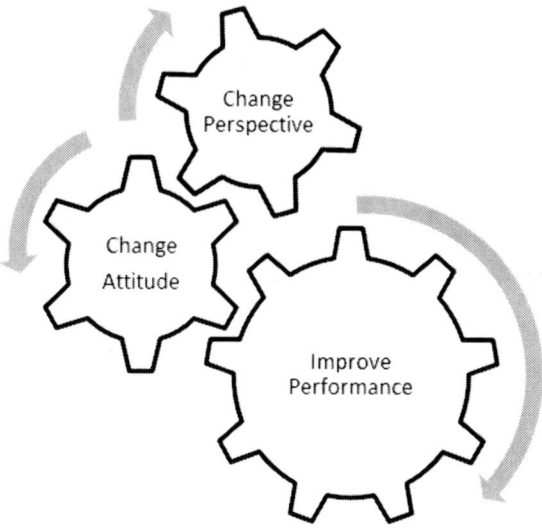

Figure 5.1

The Performance Improvement Cycle begins with changing your way of thinking. This leads to a change in attitude, and the end result or byproduct is an improvement in performance. As you can see in Figure 5.1, each phase is interrelated and dependent upon the other in order to make each wheel move. You can compare it to the inner- workings of a non-digital clock. As each wheel moves, so do the hands of the clock. As each wheel moves in the process, you'll start to see changes in your perspective, attitude, and performance. The exciting thing about this is that others will see it also! How do you begin to change not only your performance but also that of your team? I've separated it into 3 phases:

Transform Yourself
Transform your Staff
Transform your Environment (Chapter 6)

Transform Yourself

John Maxwell stated, "Change the leader, change the organization."[5] In order to transform yourself, you have to change the way in which you think. Are you a person that looks at a glass of water as being half-full or half-empty? Do you focus on what went wrong or what went right? Do you first look to criticize or compliment? Do you look for positives or negatives?

Your perspective is a direct reflection of how you think. Your first challenge is to change the way you think. Is it impossible? No. Is it difficult? Yes, but it is a fight worth fighting! The payoff is huge and will change your destiny.

Personal Change Cycle

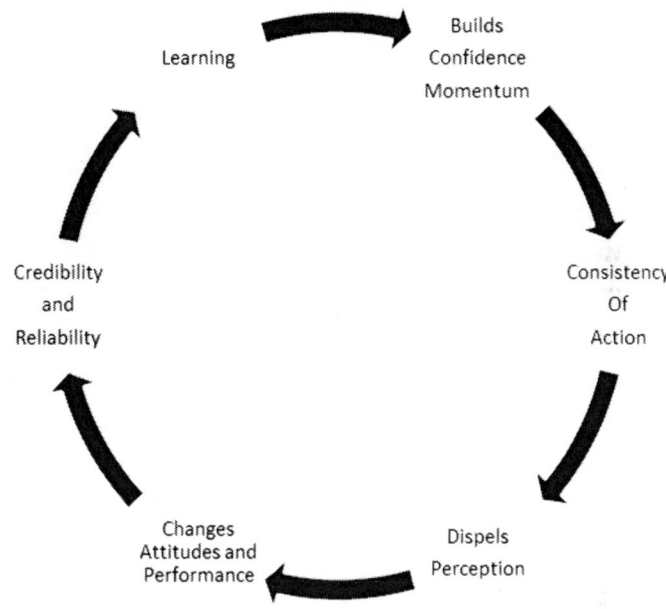

Figure 5.2

The personal change cycle begins with learning. Ken Blanchard points out in *The Heart of a Leader*, "Today, the skills you bring to the party constitute the only available form of job security."[6] This was stated in reference to the constant change that companies face daily. This was where I was struggling. Now, I would totally agree with him.

Blanchard also points out that "the very best leaders are learners—people who are always interested in ways to enhance their own knowledge and skills."[7] You cannot change your perspective or performance without learning. You cannot obtain new skills without learning. This takes commitment to apply what you have learned. Learning and application helps you build confidence. Do not forget the application side of the equation!

As the cycle progresses, you begin applying your newly-learned skills. The more you apply them, the more proficient you will become. As proficiency increases, so will success. This success will help you build your confidence, which will turn into momentum.

As you combine momentum with consistency of action, you will start to dispel people's perception of you. When this occurs, it changes not only your attitude and performance but also the attitude and performance of others. Why? It changes your relationship with those with whom you interact. As you maintain consistency of action, it leads to building up your credibility and reliability with those individuals you lead or interact with on a daily basis.

It also affects those individuals who are watching you from a distance. These people may be colleagues, other department heads, or representatives from other businesses that interact with your staff in some type of capacity. It could be a supplier or vendor, and the list could go on and on.

Your staff talks and interacts with people inside and outside your area of responsibility. Your improved performance will improve your relationship with your employees. This will be reflected in their relationships with those they interact with. This will increase and improve your reputation, which increases your ability to influence. Remember, influence is the essence of leadership. Your progress and improvement will inspire you to continue to learn.

That brings us full circle to where it all begins: learning. You cannot change the way you think unless you change what you are learning. You cannot change your perspective unless you change how you look at things. You accomplish this by learning new skills.

Learning builds confidence and produces an internal excitement that gives you a sense of hope and control. As you learn, grow, and apply new knowledge, you will start to internalize a new way of thinking. This new perspective will be outwardly manifested by your actions and possibly through your personality.

It has been said that, "At the end of a year, you will be the same person except for two things: the people you associate with and the books you read." There is a lot of wisdom in that statement. Most people in the predicament we are talking about simply quit learning.

> *Learning builds confidence and produces an internal excitement that gives you a sense of hope and control.*

My own transformation as previously described started with having the blinders removed as I read John G. Miller's book, *QBQ*. I followed that up by reading and working through Andy Andrews's book, *Mastering the Seven Decisions that Determine Personal Success*. That was followed by reading John C. Maxwell's book, *Developing the Leader Within You*.

My transformation continues to this day by reading books on leadership and management, listening to books on CD, and watching DVD's on similar topics. I have come to realize that learning is truly a life-long process, so I am using every type of media I can get my hands on to learn how to improve myself. By doing so, it will transform the relationships I have with my staff and colleagues. This will transform not only my environment but also their environment. So, dust off your pants, get back up, and start learning today!

Transform Your Staff

How do you transform your staff? Your staff's morale, productivity, and quality of work is directly related to your leadership and management style. By transforming yourself, you will automatically change your relationship with your staff just by how you interact with them. If you are a no-nonsense type of manager such as I was, looking to point out mistakes first instead of giving compliments, then the resulting change in those relationships will be dramatic when you make the transformation.

> *By transforming yourself, you will automatically change your relationship with your staff just by how you interact with them.*

There are several things you will have to do in order to transform your staff. The first thing you will have to do is to re-establish a bond with your staff. This means that you will have to earn their respect by your actions rather than your words. They will be watching with a skeptical eye, and they should. Why should they believe a single word you say unless they see it through your actions? They shouldn't.

This is where the 5 C's of Leadership come in to play. You may want to go back to chapter 4 and review these points of leadership. I printed them on a copy machine and displayed them in my office so that everyone would notice them. I placed them right behind where I sat so people could not help but notice. It was a way to send a message not only to my staff but also to myself. It was a daily reminder to keep me focused. Old habits are hard to break.

Another area that you will have to re-establish is your credibility. We all want to be credible, significant, taken seriously, and not seen as a joke or someone that can't be trusted. Credibility helps to add value to our work. In the end, this gives us the feeling of worth and self-fulfillment we all long for. I refer to this as the "Credibility Continuum."

Credibility Continuum

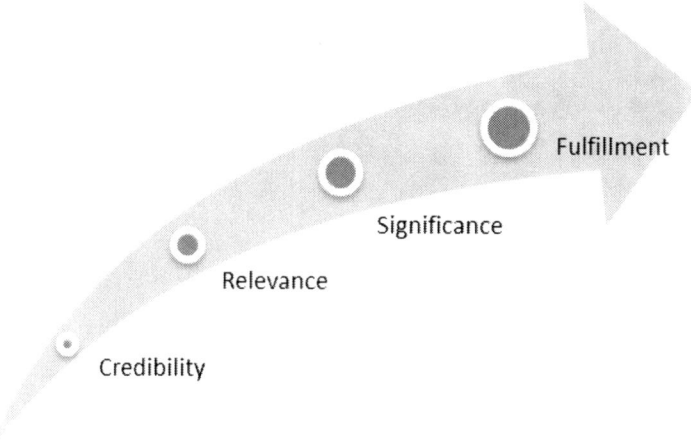

Figure 5.3

The continuum begins by establishing your credibility. This can only be done by matching what you say with what you do. Consistency between your words and actions will be used by those you lead to determine your credibility.

As your credibility increases, so does your relevance. As you become more relevant, you become more significant, which brings a feeling of self-fulfillment. This produces satisfaction related to your job and to what you are trying to accomplish. Without credibility, you cannot achieve the most satisfying thing about anyone's job and that is being self-fulfilled by the work you do.

> *The simple and most effective way to add value to someone or make someone feel valued is to visit with them.*

Remember, people want three things out of work: to be acknowledged, thus feeling valued; affirmation, knowing their work has meaning; and to add value. You are no different from your employees. You want those same things. Credibility can only be re-established through the 5 C's of Leadership. Consistency of action (Figure 5.2) will play a major role in the re-establishment process.

Your credibility can only be improved by improving the relationships with your staff. This will be key to transforming your staff and to achieving success. How do you improve your relationships with your staff? How do you re-establish that bond or make that connection I mentioned earlier? How do you improve their morale while influencing their performance? Focus on 3 key areas:

- Visit with each staff member
- Change area of focus from negative to positive feedback
- Be consistent

Visit with each staff member – What are we saying here? What we are saying is get out of the office, if you have one, and start taking time out every day or week to visit with each team member. I mean every team member, especially the ones you do not like. This one simple gesture, if done correctly, will do more to influence your staff and change your environment than anything else you will do. The most simple and effective way to add value to someone or make someone feel valued is to visit with them. Remember the 30-second rule I mentioned back in Chapter 3? This is when you say something encouraging to a person within the first 30 seconds of the conversation. I can't help but think of an old biblical proverb: "Pleasant words are a honeycomb, sweet to the soul and healing to the bones."[8]

The 30-second rule is a great way to establish or re-establish that crucial connection between you and your staff in order to change their perception of you. It seems simple, but it is also very powerful. When done consistently, the payoff is huge. In fact, you will soon start to see your staff smile when they see you. Soon, they will start asking you how you are doing. Some will even beat you to the punch by using the 30-second rule before you do. I have found this to be one of the most important tools when connecting with staff.

When visiting, do not just stop by to say "hello" and keep on moving. What you say and do during the visit is crucial to making that connection or to re-establishing the bond that will be the basis for transforming your culture, your workplace environment, and your organization. The visit should address the three things that people want out of work: to be acknowledged, to know that their work has meaning, and to know that they are adding value. By visiting with them, you accomplish the first two. Developing and training those you lead covers the third.

This brings us to the context and substance of the visit. As part of acknowledging the person, tell them how much they are needed or how important they are to the team and to the organization. Let them know that you couldn't do it without them.⁹ This clarifies how they are adding value. This helps you to start acknowledging and affirming them. Ask them how they are doing, and then *listen to them*. Let me repeat that one more time: *listen to them.* I mean, really listen to what they are saying. This will help you discern the third area employees want addressed: the opportunity to add value.

If they have a complaint, thank them for sharing it with you. Write it down, and then be sure to follow up on it. More importantly, let them know what you did or are doing to address their concern. This lets them know that you are not there for a side show.

At first, they may not choose to share anything with you except niceties, and that is okay, but do not let it deter you. Get out there every day or week, and make it a part of your routine. As they get used to seeing you visit, they'll start sharing with you things that need to be addressed. This is why you should schedule regular times to visit with your employees. The key is to do it consistently. Remember, consistency of action produces credibility and reliability.

These visits will give you a glimpse of what employees are experiencing in their environment. As time goes on, you will get to know them to a degree you never thought possible. With subsequent visits, ask them to tell you their stories and how they came to work at your organization.[10] Find out what their interests are, both at work and outside of work. Get to know their situations and their families. How many kids or grandkids do they have? What hobbies do they enjoy?

The visits show that you are genuinely interested in them and their well-being. It gives you a point of reference to start relating to your staff, thus adding more value to them as team members. It will also give you great information as to what makes them tick. This will help *you* give *them* opportunities to use their strengths to help the team. As trust develops, they will start to seek you out to help with issues and even offer suggestions as to how things could run more smoothly.

As I told you about my experience when I managed the Medical Surgical ICU, I initially visited once to twice a day. In the beginning, the staff members were reluctant to share their stories with me. As they saw me day in and day out, they opened up and started sharing their experiences, both good and bad. This gave me an opportunity to influence and shape their work environment.

One staff member shared her news of engagement with me and was excited that I stopped for a minute to talk with her about it. As time went on, when I found myself feeling down, I would go out and visit with the staff. I found that they would inspire me by telling me how they were positively impacting lives and overcoming difficult situations and obstacles. I saw them in action and the good work that was being done. I found that they made just as much of a positive impact on me as I was trying to make on them.

> *As time went on, when I found myself feeling down, I would go out and visit with the staff. I found that they would inspire me by telling me how they were positively impacting lives and overcoming difficult situations and obstacles.*

It was not long before they would see my light on in the office and stop by to chat, sharing their stories about situations they had handled or about their family life, school, and so on. Some would introduce me to loved ones who were visiting, which further cemented our relationship. I keep those memories to this day. They are special times to say the least, experiences to be savored.

Some even asked me to write reference letters so they could further their education, get into anesthesia school, and get into leadership positions. The thought of staff seeing me in this light was quite humbling. Think of the trust involved with this type of request. Requests such as these are some of the most satisfying times one can experience as a leader.

I found that the most effective visits were kept relatively short: five minutes or less. Though, if an employee wanted to talk a little longer, I would oblige. When this oc-curs, be sure to take the time to talk with them. This shows you are making progress. If it seemed like it was very im-portant to them and would take a long time, I would schedule a time to meet with them. Sometimes, we would just stop, go back to the office, and meet right then. After finishing, I would rearrange my day to make sure that I vis-ited with the other employees. Was I always successful? For the most part, I was because I made it a priority and stuck with it.

I also kept the visits lighthearted and tried to make sure that, what-ever came up, I remained positive. I also want to emphasize that the in-formation gained from these visits helped me keep a pulse on what needed to be addressed. It helped me to stay connected to what the em-ployees had to deal with or to overcome in order to do their jobs, thus help me meet their needs. To help transform your work environment, this is a necessary connection that needs to be established.

> *This will be your most difficult chal-lenge because now you are talking about applying your new perspec-tive and putting it into action.*

Change from a negative to a positive focus – This will be your most difficult challenge because now you're talking about applying your new perspective and putting it into action. It was difficult for me, and I still struggle with this at times.

As you are out and about, visiting with your staff, stop and compliment them when you observe them doing something well. As I visited the staff, I would be very attentive to what the staff was doing. When they stopped for a moment or had a break, I would visit with them. Then, I would compliment them on the good work I had seen them doing. Sometimes, it was a minor thing; sometimes, it was major. As one staff member told me, "You know, I'm starting to feel a little bit special."

I found, by and large, employees are uncomfortable getting compliments and positive feedback. They greatly appreciate it. At the same time, they really don't know how to react. Maybe its human nature, but I think it is a sad commentary on the way we manage and lead our employees.

If you have supervisors who help manage your staff, start including them on these visits. Model the behavior you want them to perform. Show them how to interact with the staff and what you want recognized.

Initially, I visited staff with my supervisors at least once a day. This was usually later in the shift. We would engage the charge nurses to find out who was the top performer of the day. We would then go over and tell the employee their charge nurse thought they were the top performer of the day. They were surprised, speechless, and would usually blush, but they were always thankful.

After a while, we would start delivering little pick-me-ups to the staff members (i.e. Starbuck's Frappuccinos®, IZZE® Raspberry drinks, Mango Ice tea, chocolate bars, etc.). We didn't do it all the time because it was the praise and recognition that was most important. As we did this day in and day out, the staff began to expect us to visit them. Soon, I started letting the supervisor take the lead, and I would chime in when appropriate. On one visit, an employee asked, "What does it take to get one of those drinks?" This proved to me the employees were paying attention to what we were doing and wanted in on it.

Be Consistent – As you are now aware, consistency is part of the 5C's of Leadership. It is such an important leadership trait that I cannot overemphasize its importance in helping you transform your workplace environment.

Consistency will build the foundation for your relationship with your staff. By and large, we are very forgiving of ourselves because we judge what we do by our intentions. However, your staff will judge you by your actions. If the two do not match up, problems will arise quickly. Your staff will rally around you and trust you if you are consistent. If you lack consistency, they will not trust you and may desert you.

> *Consistency will build the foundation for your relationship with your staff.*

I believe people have an innate yearning for consistency in their lives. They want to know what to expect so they will have some sort of control or preparation in how to react. It helps decrease stress in their lives, and we all yearn for that. So many people have trouble dealing with the constant changes in the workplace (i.e. new technology). Your relationship with your staff is no different, so strive to be consistent.

In the next chapter, we will discuss the third area of focus regarding the transformative process: transforming your environment. We will also highlight two models for coaching improved performance and the philosophy behind them, which will help you with this process.

CHAPTER 6

TRANSFORMING YOUR ENVIRONMENT

Transforming an environment can be a daunting task, even for the most experienced of leaders. It can be quite overwhelming, leaving some to wonder where they should begin.

Changing a culture happens in three distinct steps for both leadership and staff: learning, application, and consistency. Learning changes perspective and improves skills. Application improves performance. Consistency improves quality and transforms your culture. All three add value to the leadership, staff, and the organization. These areas will need to be cultivated through your leadership.

When I talk about transforming your environment, I'm not talking about facilities, equipment, cleanliness, or the attractiveness of the surroundings. These all contribute to the overall workplace experience and should not be discounted. We know certain things are also mandated by federal and state governments. This is not what I am addressing here. What I'm speaking about is the environment or culture in which you work.

If all of the above were so important to the workplace environment, my former place of business would be a pristine example for the world to follow. We were blessed to have facilities I considered second to none. In fact, many people, when visiting the facility, were stunned by its beauty and technology.

Ironically, our unit sorely lacked this same beauty. Though it was occasionally renovated, the unit was based on 1970's architecture, spatially cramped, and had not been redesigned or enlarged since its inception. It was a constant challenge we had to overcome, especially when families would compare us to the newer parts of the hospital.

Expectations had to be managed for those who were in our care. We had to instill a confidence in them that they were indeed in the right place during this crucial time in their life. Our staff did a great job setting the tone and managing those expectations. The workplace environment can help you overcome such obstacles and barriers.

I define the workplace environment as the collective attitude of your employees. This attitude includes equipping those you lead with the skills to perform effectively. I know it seems like a simplistic definition, but it is here where you'll find success or failure. In fact, it's so simple that we as leaders sometimes forget to give it the attention it deserves.

We tend to focus on the physical aspects of our chosen professions and fields of business. We look at technology, computer systems, machinery, and how much we are wired up. We think in terms of cost, productivity, profits, and capital investments. We hire consultants to perform feasibility studies, reorganize organizational structures, and reorganize reporting relationships all under the guise of realignment and cost-containment. We hire management engineers to perform productivity studies to streamline processes to make the company more efficient. Again, I'm not saying these are not important endeavors in our highly competitive industries.

What I have seen from study after study and consultant after consultant is they continue to miss the one thing that makes all of this work: from the top on down, they miss or overlook the fact that it's about the people. A key element to transforming your workplace environment is the development of positive relationships with your staff.

You can reorganize all you want, change who reports to whom, and buy all of the new equipment you can afford. However, you cannot apply that mentality to the relationships you have with your employees. It simply won't and doesn't work that way. These are your employees, and the relationships you build with them will determine your success or failure. This is because their attitude and motivation to do a good job will reflect that relationship.

I sit back and wonder sometimes how much inefficiency, lack of production, and low morale has been directly related to well-intentioned reorganization efforts that sacrificed effective reporting relationships.

The good news is that, once you've transformed yourself, you will forever change the relationships you have with your staff. This one change will also start to change the relational dynamics between your employees. The resulting transformation of your workplace environment will then be a byproduct directly related to your relationship with each staff member.

If you believe as I do that a team's attitude is a mere reflection of their leader, you will understand that the collective attitude of your employees will be reflective of your leadership style. If you are positive, uplifting, and genuinely value your employees through words and actions, you'll have a highly motivated workforce with a positive workplace environment.

> *Do you have enough courage to put your ego aside to develop those relationships?*

Morale, productivity, and teamwork will reawaken because your employees will start to be acknowledged, knowing their work has meaning. In turn, this will help them to feel like valuable members of the team. When this occurs, employee ownership will be born and will take hold, thus transforming the culture and workplace environment.

The key, regardless of what level of leadership you are in, is to develop positive relationships with your staff, building on the 5C's of Leadership. This can only occur through the efforts of one person, the person you greet in the mirror each day.

The question and challenge then becomes, "Do you have enough courage to put your ego aside to develop those relationships?" If you've gotten this far, I believe you do!

NEGATIVITY – RUINATION OF THE WORKPLACE

Have you ever been talking to someone, and all they did was complain about this and complain about that? And… nothing they said had any positive value to it. Do you remember how exhausted you were after the experience? If you weren't exhausted, it's probably because you cut it short and got yourself out of earshot of the offending party. Or, when talking to that individual, you found yourself thinking of something else, nodding at the appropriate times, and hoping they would soon bring the conversation to a close. This probably led you to avoid that person in the future. In short, they sapped you of your energy and negatively affected your morale.

I find that negativity in the workplace is like a cancer that can spread if left unchecked. Negative people find a type of empowerment that fills a void through a negative self-image that is expressed by their negativity. They are genuinely unhappy people who are intent on making others unhappy. The sadness of it all is that some do not even recognize it. They don't have a clue or do not care about the impact their attitudes have on their fellow colleagues or work environment. To them, it's always someone else's problem to deal with. They create a self-fulfilling prophecy.

According to David Cottrell, President of Cornerstone Leadership, "You cannot afford to have negative people on your team. Negative people drain your energy, destroy your confidence, and slash your productivity."[1] He also makes the case that a negative person seems to have a greater influence than the positive one. Anecdotally, I would agree.

Why do I recognize and despise all of this negativity? Because, I was there and left many people miserable in my wake. It is sort of like the alcoholic who, after going through rehab, sees the results of past behaviors and looks at them with disdain. Once rehabilitated, these people know the destructive nature of the disease and the harm it did to everyone around them, and this is why they hold it in such contempt. Granted, this is not to equate alcoholism with negativity. One clearly bears a cost the other does not. The parallel I'm drawing here is that the negative person, just like the alcoholic, will try to bring down everyone he or she encounters if left unchecked.

Thankfully, I woke up one day as previously described. Today, I cannot stand to be around negative people. I do not associate with them, nor do I pay too much attention to them, other than when I have to interact with them. When this happens, I always try to make it a positive encounter.

What did I mean by not paying them too much attention? Did I mean ignore them? Nope. Did I mean avoid them? Surely not! As a leader, you can't. So, what did I mean? I mean that you should visit with them just as anyone else. You should counter everything they point out as a negative and turn it into a positive. Sometimes, you have to point out the obvious in the most simplistic of terms (i.e. "At least we have a job to be thankful for."). Strive to make every encounter a positive one.

> *As a leader, you have to make sure you never buy into their negativity. Doing so will only empower and embolden them.*

You can also diminish their influence by the relationships you build with the other employees you lead. As a leader, you have to make sure you never buy into their negativity. Doing so will only empower and embolden them. You always get what you reward. By not rewarding that type of behavior, they will either change their behavior or leave to make someone else miserable. The point is not to let them dominate your time, your thinking, or your actions.

One of our up-and-coming nurses told me a story about a new nurse that had transferred into the unit. She would jokingly but consistently say negative things during their shift about various subjects. One night, he overheard another nurse explain to the new nurse that they really didn't do the negative thing in this department, and maybe she needed to look for a new place to work if she didn't like it here.

This nurse smiled from ear to ear, telling me how good it felt to hear those words of wisdom being spoken because his colleagues prided themselves on their atmosphere of teamwork. This incident demonstrates how the collective attitude of the team protects itself from the torments of the negative person.

As I told our staff at my first staff meeting, "Life is not like math, where multiplying two negatives equals a positive. It simply doesn't work that way." I told them to not engage or hang around negative people because nothing good would ever come from it. What negative people do not understand is that their success is based on positive relationships, and the more people they drive away by their negativity, the fewer opportunities they will have to succeed.

The last thing I would say regarding the negative employee is to set the expectation of the appropriate attitude they'll need to display if they choose to continue working for you. Point out the impact of their behavior, the correct behavior that should be displayed, and the consequences of not displaying said behavior. Expect passive aggressiveness and the manipulation of events, but rely on documentation and direct coaching sessions to combat such behavior.

The best way to end negative behavior is through direct coaching, and you can only do that by engaging the employee. Through coaching, you can help the employee learn the appropriate ways to get problems addressed. They either will conform or move on, either by their choice or yours.

You also have to differentiate between a chronic complainer and an employee who deeply cares but is frustrated. These employees can still be salvaged with some good coaching. I have found that these people, once turned, can be a great asset to the team. Many times, they get a bum rap, are disregarded, and are branded as "complainers" or "not team players." To be honest, what they really need from us as managers and leaders is to meet their needs and expectations. Sometimes, we forget it is a two-way street! So, *listen* carefully to what they are saying before you start judging them.

> *Many managers choose to leave negative people alone. When this occurs, their behavior has been sanctioned appropriate by default.*

In summary, negativity can be very frustrating and difficult to deal with. Many managers choose to leave negative people alone. When this occurs, their behavior has been sanctioned appropriate by default.

If negativity is left unchecked, it will destroy your workplace environment. Always be on the lookout for negativity, and when it does rear its ugly head, first look at yourself to see if it's something you've failed to do, explain, or communicate. Then, look at the employee, engage them as soon as possible, and turn it into a positive. You can do this by either coaching them to improve their performance or by helping them to move on.

Our obligation to each employee is to provide them with an environment where they can be successful. But remember, the collective attitude of your team is your workplace environment. When one of the team members continues to detract from the team and refuses to change, your obligation is strictly to the team. Give them a chance to change, and if they don't, move them out as soon as possible. Your team doesn't deserve to carry that burden.

HIRING FOR SUCCESS – ATTITUDE VERSUS EXPERIENCE

There are differing viewpoints on what type of person you should hire. These viewpoints can be separated into two camps: those that advocate for attitude and those for experience. One of our nation's foremost authorities on leadership, John C. Maxwell, has even changed his position over time. His has evolved from the attitude camp and now gravitates more toward the experience side.

When I took over the leadership of managing our Medical Surgical Intensive Care Unit, I identified certain areas of focus that our leadership team needed to address. Among them were the hiring, orientation, and training of our employees. We needed to hire the right type of employee and put them through a great orientation process to help build the foundation for them and the team to succeed. This began with hiring the right type of people, organizing the people we already had, and putting the right people in the right places doing the right things.[2] Our orientation program became recognized as a best practice within our hospital. Several departments within our hospital sought us out, adopting and adapting different parts of our orientation program to meet their needs. We also partnered with one of our sister hospitals to help orient their nurses to critical care.

The hiring and effective on-boarding of employees helped to drive the transformation of our workplace envi-

> *The hiring and effective on-boarding of employees helped to drive the transformation of our workplace environment.*

ronment. It will also drive yours. It's an intentional and focused process. This won't happen overnight because it's a process of constant evaluation and re-evaluation, matching people's skill sets with performance.

Coming from the old school, I tended to look at experience first and foremost when hiring individuals. I was so caught up in it prior to my transformation. I wouldn't even interview people from outside of our hospital system. This was based on what I believed was solid evidence.

Let me tell you a funny story about my former boss that I still get a kick out of to this day. I once had an applicant apply for a job with our office, Nursing Administration. She was coming from a prestigious hospital, but I wouldn't even talk to her or accept her application. I had a blanket rule of not hiring people from outside our system because they did not have the internal operational experience I thought was necessary to effectively do the job. I viewed it as a waste of my time. Seven years later, we had a change in our leadership, and I got a new boss, and who do you think that was? Yep, you guessed it. It was the applicant that I refused to even grant an interview.

When we first met, she had not forgotten the incident and promptly reminded me of the occurrence. Being somewhat slow of speech but quick of wit, I immediately told her, "You wouldn't be where you are today if I hadn't made that decision." We both laughed and over the years, I can honestly say that she was the best boss I have ever worked for. It was all based on an assumption that was wrong even though I eventually benefited from it. Carol Moody went on to become the South Carolina Nurse Leader of the Year for 2013. Talk about missing the boat! It was the best bad decision I ever made.

> *The decision to hire someone to replace or expand your staff is critical to the overall success of the team and environment.*

The decision to hire someone to replace or expand your staff is critical to the overall success of the team and environment. You're about to introduce someone into the team who will change the team's dynamics. Their success will be related directly to how well the new employee adapts to the new environment, learns the skills needed to succeed, and meshes or blends in with the team.

Treat this process with respect because the team's success will be affected by the type of person you hire. The stakes are pretty high, and many compromise their standards. They let the pressure of time and the need to fill the position overwhelm them into making a bad decision. The resulting carnage and havoc wrought is usually devastating. This erodes the staff's confidence in their leader.

In the end, you'll have to make a decision and choose a direction. Being from the old school, I had always advocated for experience. After my own transformation and seeing the positive effects of attitude on performance, I made the choice to change and emphasize the attitude side of the equation. How can one attempt to transform a culture or improve performance while hiring negative people? You can't and won't!

HIRE FOR ATTITUDE – YOU CAN TEACH SKILL

I believe adamantly that you should hire for attitude. Let me state that again: HIRE FOR ATTITUDE! I just want to be crystal clear on this point. Why? I have found that you can't teach attitude like you can skill. Attitude is simply too strong of a determinant in an individual's success.

I can hear all of the questions coming forth in disagreement. What about experience? Should you simply disregard experience? Let's be very clear on that point also: NO. Let's say that again so that we can be fair to both sides: NO!

The best of both worlds is good attitude and good experience. That is what you should look for first and foremost. The second is good attitude and good skill. Skill and experience are two different things and should not be confused with each other. Experience is utilizing or applying specific skills over a period of time while skill is knowledge that enables someone to get the job done.

The third is good attitude and good aptitude, meaning the candidate has the *ability to learn* the skills in order to be a successful team member. Attitude is not everything, but you'll notice that in every one of the three instances I gave, experience was only mentioned in the first one. "Good attitude" was mentioned in all three. A good attitude is mentally-driven. Experience, skill, and aptitude are performance-driven.

Over the years, I have seen numerous candidates with outstanding experience but with such horrible attitudes that it totally negated their value as employees. We have treated experience with such high reverence that we have elevated it to almost an entitlement for procuring a job. As previously stated, there are varying viewpoints on this subject matter, but I base my opinion on what I have seen work in the workplace environment. Let us review the priorities of hiring one more time:

1. Good Attitude and Good Experience
2. Good Attitude and Good Skill
3. Good Attitude and Good Aptitude

When hiring, make sure that you have identified the type of skill sets you desire for the performance of the job. If you do not have a job description, develop one. Be specific concerning the duties to be performed, minimum qualifications, etc. Decide on what skill mix should be included, and don't forget that the ability to relate to team members and respond appropriately to feedback are skills just as important as other technical skills.

As previously stated, the hiring process was an area of focus for our leadership team. We saw that the standardized interview tools were not meeting our needs, so we developed our own interview tools. We implemented a phone interview tool used to screen appropriate applicants and a face-to-face interview tool for those we called for follow-up interviews. We implemented behavioral interviewing based on Martin Yate's *Hiring the Best*.[3]

Develop a template of questions that includes a numerical scoring system. This will help you rank order your applicants. Keep the scoring system simple (i.e. a scale of one to five with *one* being the worst and *five* being the best). Ask both skill- and situational-related questions. Situational questions elicit behavioral responses. This is behavioral interviewing. By asking situational or behavioral questions during the interview, you'll have a good idea of how the person will react during key situations.

> When "Good Attitude" combines with "Good Performance," you'll have a win-win situation.

When "Good Attitude" combines with "Good Performance," you'll have a win-win situation. It makes the "cream of the crop" rise to the top.

Heavily pre-screen applicants prior to bringing them in for a face-to-face interview. We did a tremendous amount of phone interviewing prior to selecting those for face-to-face interviews.

When conducting face-to-face interviews, have several frontline team members, along with yourself, interview the candidates. This will constitute your team member interview panel. I must say that I was very skeptical when the idea was first introduced by the Studer organization at one of our hospital's quarterly leadership meetings. The more I thought about it, the more I liked it. What other way is there to show confidence in your staff than to empower them to help choose their teammates and reshape your culture? I can't think of another way. Can you?

There is one caveat: the staff interview panel should be made up of high performers committed to the team's vision and success. In other words, keep cynics and negative people off of these panels. As a leadership team, we committed to this process and had great success with it.

As the leader, you should interview the candidates separately from the team member panel. This is done to remove any biases that your presence may bring. Have each panelist score independently without comparing notes. This type of interview process reminds me of another proverb which states, "Where there is no guidance, the people fall, but in abundance of counselors, there is victory."[4]

After the interviews, in a forum with the team member panel, discuss openly the pros and cons of each applicant. This will give you a chance to compare your interview with that of the panel and come to a consensus. Compare the scores of everyone involved in the interview process. We also averaged each applicant's score, which helped to place them in rank order. This will help you make an unemotional decision regarding which applicants to bring back for a second interview or which to offer the job.

As a note of caution, rank ordering is only a tool to help you in the selection process. It should not be the ultimate deciding factor. A candidate may rank high but may not fit in very well with the team and vice versa.

Generally speaking, the highest rank-ordered applicant will usually be the one who will seem to meet the needs of the team the most. If you have more than one position open, use it to offer multiple candidates a job. Depending on your organization's policy, this may or may not require another set of interviews.

If they didn't make it the first time around, that doesn't mean they're not a match to help you succeed. Sometimes, it's the depth of the interview pool; other times, it's timing. We had several individuals come back one and two years later to interview after heeding our advice to sharpen their skills before applying again. They were in very deep interview pools, but their attitude and willingness to learn and accept advice made them great additions to our team! This proved that we made the entire interview process a positive experience even when an individual didn't make it onto the team the first time.

We had great results with this process. Again, do not treat it trivially or hurriedly. It is too important. It will also give you the best chance at bringing in quality individuals because, after all, the team you're leading deserves that. It does take time, but it's time well spent. You can use this process to reshape your workplace environment and continue supplementing the team with quality players for long-term success.

You also will get input from your employees because they, too, want good team members and to be involved in choosing them. Giving them a stake in the process adds tremendous value to them, and the resulting payoff is huge with multiple benefits for the department and organization. It creates ownership of a shared vision.

Keep the size of the team member interview panel to no more than three or four people, if possible. We found that panels larger than this were overwhelming to the applicants and negatively affected their interviews.

> *Giving them a stake in the process adds tremendous value to them, and the resulting payoff is huge with multiple benefits for the department and organization. It creates ownership of a shared vision.*

Keep in mind that some candidates are interview savvy, which may be deceiving. These people are difficult to spot. If your gut is telling you the person is not a good fit, or you get bad vibes, listen to what your gut is telling you. If you're experiencing this, some on your interview panel will also. I believe we all have a discerning spirit, and we would do well to listen to it when it speaks to us.

PERFORMANCE BASED COACHING

Another key to transforming your environment is the development of your employees. We totally rebuilt our staff orientation and education program. Performance is easier to coach when the employee is provided with a solid foundation from which to start. I could write a whole book on performance-based coaching, but for the purposes of this book, we will concentrate on two models we used to coach our employees.

A key to coaching for improved performance is to make it timely and consistent. Giving timely and consistent feedback will not only enhance your employees' performance, but it will add to your credibility as a manager and leader. Noted management and leadership expert, Ken Blanchard, points out that "what keeps performance going and helps achieve the goals is day-to-day coaching. Unfortunately, this is the step in the performance management system that is missing in most organizations."[5]

> *By focusing on performance, you stay away from emotional issues that can hinder learning, thus preventing changes in behavior and performance.*

As you engage in coaching sessions, your employees will see by your actions that you care enough to help *them* to succeed—as well as the organization. Maintaining a positive emphasis will lay the foundation and set the atmosphere for the employees, allowing them to apply what they have learned. This will help them rise to meet the standards or expectations that have been set. Your responsibility is to coach from a positive point of view. Theirs is to apply what has been coached.

By focusing on performance, you stay away from emotional issues that can hinder learning, thus preventing changes in behavior and performance. Share with the staff that you'll be implementing this type of coaching so they can see immediately that you are serious about raising the team's performance to a higher level. Be open about it, and explain it to them.

Let them know the circumstances in which coaching sessions will occur. When the occasion arises, let them know you need to have a coaching session with them. This frames the conversation in the right context. This way, the employee can start preparing mentally to be an active participant in the session and not a passive listener.

Let us now turn our attention to the nuts and bolts of improving performance.

On-Time Coaching

We have discussed complimenting people when you visit with them, utilizing the 30-second rule. How can we take learning opportunities or mistakes and turn them into positive situations and experiences our employees?

I use the Praise-Feedback-Praise technique (PFP). I also use a model I call the Performance Review Model. Both of these are types of "On-time Coaching" used to quickly address behavioral or process-driven issues. These should be documented and placed in the employee's file. This will help track performance and address the concerns of your human resources department when performance issues arise. We developed a standard form for this purpose. This documentation serves a dual purpose: to help good employees improve their performance and to help you move low performers out. This will be a win-win situation for the team.

We need to be fair to the employee and coach them toward better performance. We are responsible for developing them for the good of the team and the organization. Employees can't address performance issues unless they know about it. As Ken Blanchard pointed out, many fail in this area. I believe this is unethical. Based on my experience, most employees appreciate the coaching and will strive to meet the standard of performance if presented in a positive manner.

Praise-Feedback-Praise (PFP = Behavior Focused)

Praise – Find something positive and encouraging to say about the employee. This sets the tone for the conversation to come. It also gives them a feeling of worth and value. It may be as simple as thanking them showing up to work every day and explaining how much you actually need them. Be sure that the praise is honest and sincere.

If there is nothing you can find to praise, or if the situation is such that praise is not appropriate, do not praise them. Move on to the feedback part of the discussion, and proceed from there. Praise must be sincere and genuine; otherwise, the employees will see through it.

Feedback – Tell them about the situation and what concerns you have about their performance. Tell them how it has impacted the team, department, business, or as in our case, patient care.

Praise – This is where you state the level of performance you expect from the person. It is also where you instill confidence in his or her ability to improve performance, attitude, or whatever it is you are addressing.

Performance Review Model (PRM = Process Focused)

Ask the employee the following questions:

What did you do well? This mentally focuses the employee on their positive actions. It puts their mind in a state where learning can take place. Start from a positive.

What should have occurred? This gets the employee to think operationally as to what should have occurred so the problem could have been avoided.

What can you do better? This gets the employee to think about how they can match their actions to what you expect.

By focusing on process, you take all emotion out of the equation. In doing so, you help the employee focus on what should have occurred. It helps the employee stay out of the "Gotcha" syndrome, which inhibits learning and performance.

Some may ask, "What if the employee didn't do anything right?" Or, "What if they can't identify what they did correctly?" If that's the case, start at the second step: "What should have occurred?" As you review the process with the person, you can point out to the employee what he or she did correctly. This helps the employee reaffirm that he or she did something right, minimizing the negative effects of the review.

People learn best in a positive environment, so mine the positives as much as you can. Regardless of which method you use, the employee should clearly understand the new performance expectations by the time the conversation has ended.

> *If an employee is simply not measuring up to the standards that you have set after numerous attempts to turn them around, then it's time to have a different type of conversation.*

I use both methods. I primarily use the Praise-Feedback-Praise model to coach behavioral or disciplinary issues, and I use the Performance Review Model for process-based issues. You may combine them, depending on the situation. This is not uncommon. Sometimes, behavioral concerns cause problems with process-based performance.

If an employee is simply not measuring up to the standards that you have set after numerous attempts to turn them around, then it's time to have a different type of conversation. What you are talking about here is whether or not the team benefits from keeping the employee. In other words, is the person causing more trouble than he or she is worth? Is the person starting to detract or take away from the value of the team?

These are serious cases because you're talking about someone's livelihood, but you also have to keep the team's interest at the forefront. The team's success is dependent upon your actions. In this case, bring the employee in and have a professional but frank discussion. This is not a time to listen to excuses from the employee. You are beyond that point. Explain to the person that, based on his or her actions and performance, it seems that he or she does not want to be a part of the team. At this time, you have two choices: either put the person on a performance-improvement plan with definite performance expectations along with a timeline in which to accomplish said expectations, or you can let the person go. As always, be sure to document these conversations, and work with your human resources representative if you have one.

Consistency – Are you beginning to see how crucial consistency is to what you do on a daily basis? Many do not because they do not pay it the attention it deserves and are left wondering why the staff mistrusts them as much as they do. These leaders simply do not understand the link between consistency and credibility. Without consistency, you'll have no credibility with your staff because you will not be seen as a reliable person.

In your coaching, strive to be consistent with all of your employees. When inconsistency occurs in this area, other staff will assume that you are playing the game of favoritism. This will not only sacrifice your credibility, but it will also harm morale. Remember, this is an area where you'll be judged strictly from the employee's point of view.

We've gone over a lot of material, so let's summarize the key areas of focus for transforming your staff and your environment.

The first step is to get out and visit your staff members, utilizing the 30-second rule.

The second step is to change your focus from negative to positive feedback.

The third step is to be consistent.

Other elements include performance-based coaching, addressing negativity in the workplace, and improving your team through the hiring process. An important part of that process is to hire for attitude in the following priority: good attitude, good experience; good attitude, good skill; and good attitude, good aptitude.

In closing, one cannot overemphasize the importance of consistency. Without consistency, you're spinning your wheels and wasting your time. Without it, your staff will label you as being unreliable, thus negating your ability to influence and lead. All is lost without consistency.

We will now turn our attention to "Changing a Culture." We will look at the leader's role in determining that culture, including insights into how you affect that process.

CHAPTER 7

UNDERSTANDING PERFORMANCE AND ORGANIZATIONAL CULTURE

"If you can't change the people, change the people."
-Anonymous

What did you think when you read the quote above? Let's be honest for a second. Did you think as I did that you needed to change your staff and get some new people in there? Or, did you think you needed to change the behavior, attitude, and performance of your staff? Did you immediately think that it was *you* that needed to change in order to get your staff to perform better?

I can trace my transformational journey back to the exact moment I read that quote. I first read it in a leadership meeting at work. It was an innocuous quote listed at the top of one of the papers passed around the table. It was addressed in almost a passing sense, but it caught my eye. The reason it caught my eye was because I was looking for answers. It seemed to line up with my thoughts and beliefs at the time.

What I came to realize is that the quote can be viewed in several different ways, depending on your mindset. If you look at a picture one way, it shows one type of image. When you view it from a different angle or point-of-focus, you get a totally different image.

Let's take a look at our workplace environment, the culture of that environment, and how it is shaped. We will look at the steps needed to bring balance back into the workplace and the effects of organizational structure and finance on that environment.

DESTRUCTIVE PERFORMANCE CYCLE

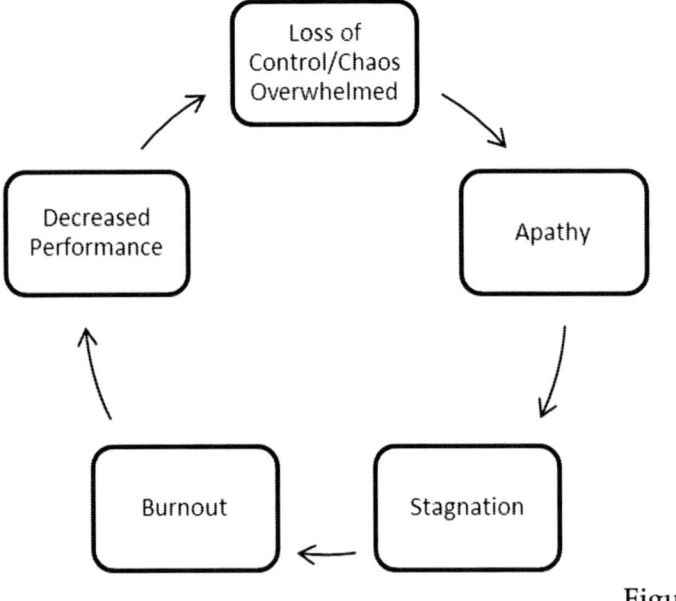

Figure 7.1

As you look at the cycle in Figure 7.1, the first step in the cascade of decreasing performance that staff will experience is a feeling of loss of control. They interpret this as chaos, which results in a feeling of being overwhelmed. If not held in check, this will lead to apathy. In turn, this will lead to stagnation. If stagnation persists, it will result in burnout. The end result is decreased performance. The cycle then repeats and deepens. Decreased performance usually occurs in each step of this destructive cycle. Recognize the steps, and be ready to address the situation at the earliest possible time.

Each employee will experience different stages at different times, and they will be affected in different ways. This is because we as individuals handle and react to stress in our own unique ways. What stresses one of us may not even show up on the radar screen of another.

During your visits with staff, you'll most likely be able to pick up on what stage your employees may be experiencing. This is one reason why a routine of visiting the staff is important to the success of the team. By constantly verifying where they are, mentally-speaking, you will position yourself to be able to coach and mentor them back to a healthy state of performance.

The earlier you engage employees in the cycle, the better it is for all involved. The major benefit to the team of such engagement is maintenance of good morale. We all struggle from time to time in everything we do, but struggles can lead to crises. In turn, this can lead to poor decisions, which can take you down a dreadful path of self-destruction.

How do we counter such cycles? Is visiting with staff the answer to everything? It's significant, but it's not everything. To understand how to change a culture within the workplace environment we need to understand the forces at work within that environment.

S<small>PHERES OF</small> B<small>ALANCE</small>

Figure 7.2

Spheres of balance are major areas of influence or forces that affect the workplace environment. The forces are made up of three areas (Figure 7.2): the overall workplace environment, the employees, and the leader. Two of the three forces are people driven: the leader and the employees. The third force, the workplace environment, is a byproduct of the first two. It represents the relationship that exists between employees and leadership.

Each force overlaps the other to one degree or another. I placed these forces in circles to demonstrate when the spheres or forces are in balance. This is represented by the middle triangle, created by the overlapping spheres. You're centered when you reach a balanced workplace environment. The middle triangle created by the spheres is where each manager or leader should strive to be. That is the goal! When the spheres are in balance, all areas are functioning according to their purpose and with the desired effect.

UNBALANCED SPHERES

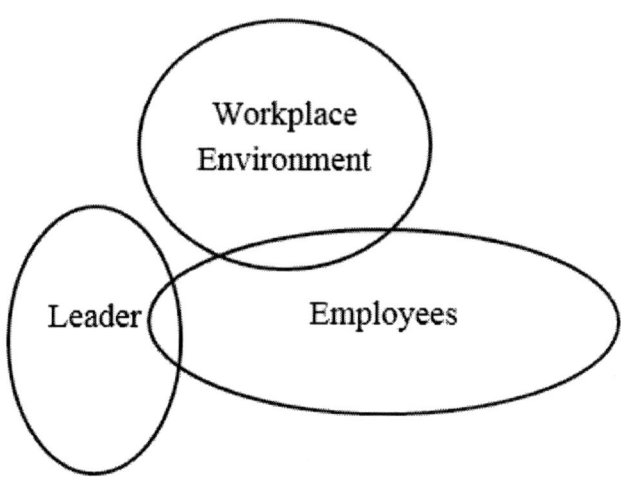

Figure 7.3

Forces can also become unbalanced or disconnected, as seen in figure 7.3. This is where problems arise within either the employee or leadership spheres, and they are the result of a deficiency. The deficiencies manifest themselves as negativity, lack of consistency, and decreased performance in the employee sphere. In the leadership sphere, these same issues result in a failure of leadership.

When unbalanced, compensatory mechanisms kick in, attempting to hold the workplace environment together in order to stay in balance. As one sphere increases to compensate, another decreases. The spheres flex up and down (increase or decrease) to meet the deficiency, depending on the affected area. Most of the time, you will see this flexing up and down within the leader and employee spheres.

As stated, these spheres are contracting and inflating constantly, based on the performance of both the leader and the employees. Remember, the workplace environment is the byproduct of the other two spheres.

Outside forces may also cause fluctuations within the spheres, such as a change in ownership, the economy, supply shortages, and so on. These are forces that you have no control over, but it's important to know how they can affect your environment.

There's an old saying, "When leadership is absent, chaos reigns." The byproduct of a lack of leadership is a poor workplace environment with sobering effects: low morale, low productivity, and low quality. The hits will just keep coming, but in this case, the lows will just keep getting lower and lower.

As the leader, you are directly responsible for all three spheres. The quality of your managerial leadership will directly influence and impact the quality of the other two spheres. It takes leadership to manage effectively. Your leadership will determine whether or not you achieve a balanced workplace environment.

MANAGEMENT BY ORGANIZATIONAL CHARTS

Every business has an organizational structure. Each structure is unique to that company. Many large company structures parallel each other (i.e. president, vice president, senior administrators, administrators, directors, managers, assistant managers, supervisors, team leaders, and last-but-not least, the frontline staff. This type of hierarchy and structure gives a full nine layers of management before we get to the frontline employee. Not all businesses have this many layers, but this is not at all unusual for large companies.

> *Hypocritically, we often place the employee at the bottom rung of the ladder, yet we expect a superior product and a great workplace environment.*

Hypocritically, we often place the frontline employees at the bottom rung of the ladder, yet we expect them to produce a superior product and workplace environment. Does this make any sense to you? I know the Bible states that the first shall be last and the last shall be first, but somehow, I don't think this is what it was talking about. It amazes me how this can be, but it happens over and over again.

Many innovative companies are changing and moving away from the traditional hierarchal structure and its top-down management culture. IDEO (pronounced "eye-dee-oh") is one such company. They are a world-renowned global design company known for their innovation and quality. According to their website, their philosophy "takes a human-centered, design-based approach to helping organizations in the public and private sectors innovate and grow."[1] They use a flat organizational structure to bring about the type of workplace environment that has produced the quality and innovation we have all benefited from: products such as NEC computer screens, Apple's first computer mouse, high-tech medical devices, and much more.

We tend to manage according to organizational charts. What do I mean by this? In the traditional, hierarchal top-down structure, you have formalized reporting structures with well-defined lines of authority and communication. Leaders, managers, and supervisors translate this structure into how they manage and relate to their employees. Adherence to the structure drives all facets of the business. If you want to do X, then you have to talk to Y. What if Y doesn't agree or does not like what is being proposed? Many companies structured this way have formalized committee structures which I heard once described as "the killing fields of ideas."

> *In the competitive world of business where the one constant is change, adherence to uniformity suppresses the ability to meet the challenges of that ever-changing environment.*

The problem with the hierarchal, top-down management structure is that it can stifle innovation due to the rigidity of that structure. Such structures produce cultures that demand uniformity instead of unity of purpose. In the competitive world of business where the one constant is change, adherence to uniformity suppresses the ability to meet the challenges of that ever-changing environment.

Ideas and innovation are halted by positional status and formalized committees. This promotes a focus on why something "can't be done" or "won't work" rather than on "what can be done to make it work." This self-imposed uniformity rule creates a constant barrier that builds frustration within the workforce for all involved, preventing the progress of the organization. This directly impacts your leadership, thus impacting your relationship with your staff. If caught in this type of structure, you will have to adapt, improvise, and overcome to move things forward.

At IDEO, they employ unity of purpose in designing solutions to bring quality products to the marketplace. By doing so, positional status and committee structures are irrelevant and are replaced with teams that focus on process. They know that when you focus on process, you'll not only get the results you want, but you'll also get quality results. This is where ideas and innovations become reality.

If you look at a traditional organizational chart, you will see that it is constructed similar to a pyramid:

Typical Organizational Chart Structure

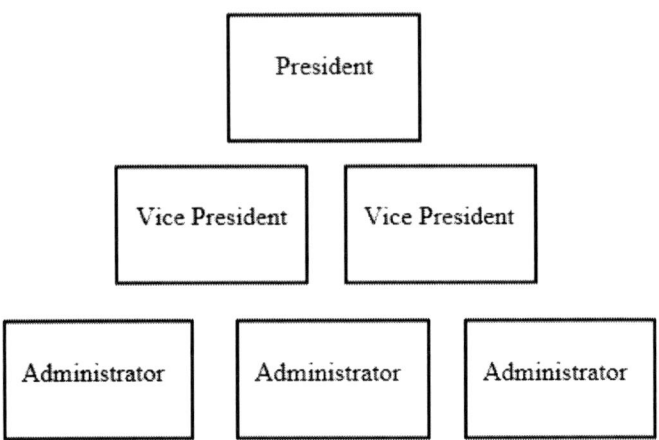

Figure 7.4

This is a typical, hierarchal and top-down management structure. To make my point, let us take the spheres of balance we discussed earlier and put them in a pyramid, and then it will become clearer as to what I mean:

Misaligned Pyramidal Organizational Structure

Figure 7.5

As you can see, the leader is at the top of the pyramid, just as it is in the organizational chart. The employees are in the next layer with the workplace environment on the bottom. In this model, what we're saying is that management is top priority, staff is somewhere in the middle or down the list of priorities, and the workplace environment is last. The workplace environment is an afterthought.

I guess we assume that if we just do X, X, and X, we'll have a great workplace environment. In other words, orders will come down from the top, moving down to the staff, who will jump through the hoops those at the top create to produce a great product. Somewhere in the process, a great workplace environment that produces excellence will be developed. In reality, it simply doesn't work that way.

This model is wrong and backwards. Organizational structures are very important. As previously discussed, they can make or break a company, based on the bureaucracy that is developed. Let's not make the mistake of translating that into how we manage and lead people.

What should be occurring? Let's take a look at what a properly aligned pyramidal organizational structure looks like:

Properly Aligned Pyramidal Organizational Structure

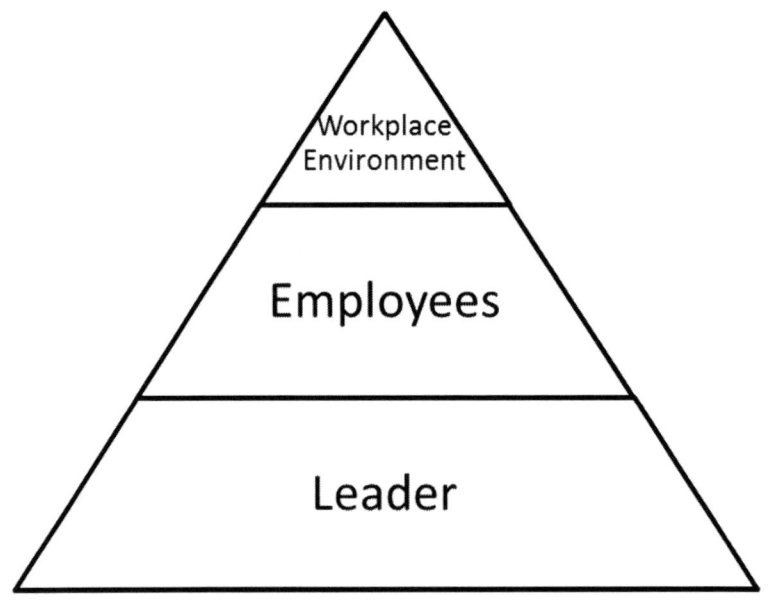

Figure 7.6

I believe that leadership should be on bottom, providing the foundation from which everything else is built. Leaders should be in direct support of the staff with a focus on enhancing the workplace environment (the collective attitude of the employees) as the top priority. This collective attitude includes *developing* the employees, thus giving them the skills to meet the demands of the job.

When the workplace environment becomes the top priority, performance improves, morale is high, and quality is second to none. This occurs because the staff becomes engaged and developed.

FINANCE – IT'S NOT ALL ABOUT THE NUMBERS

Financial resources have a part to play in all of this, so let's discuss this aspect and its effect on operations and employees. Finance affects any organizational structure and directly impacts you as a leader. Take a look at any organization's budget for staff development and training. When things get tight, this is often the first item to be cut. After all, training does indeed take money.

New York Times best-selling authors, Roger Connors and Tom Smith, discuss the importance of training in their book, *How Did That Happen: Holding People Accountable – For Results – The Positive, Principled Way.* The two have studied and consulted on leadership, management, and training for a couple of decades. They cite a study by the global management consulting company, Accenture, in which two-thirds of the leadership surveyed didn't think their employees had the skills necessary to do their jobs at industry-leading levels.[2] They also cite a study done by the American Society for Training & Development (ASTD), which found that 74 percent of workers felt they had received insufficient training. [3]

Based on these two studies, it seems as if leadership and staff are on the same page. Connors and Smith came to the conclusion that the expectations of a company are often not met due to this lack of training, so they propose making the development of employees a top priority.

Ongoing education and training for staff can be a large part of your budget. Many of you may or may not have any control over what is placed into the budget for this expense. Not all is lost if this is the case. In these challenging financial times, tough decisions have to be made when prioritizing how much to spend and to which areas those resources will be allocated. It is a tough call but one that should be handled with a full understanding of the consequences involved.

When putting together budgets, financial analysts use many different types of financial models, depending on what is being discussed. Given the topic, they do research and plug the information into those models. In turn, this gives us such things as cost-benefit analysis and market forecasts. All of this is done in hopes of increasing revenues, saving money, and adding to the profit margin.

I believe there is more than meets the eye here than simple numbers. Let me explain. Some financial analysts will say that by investing in X, you will save Y. This is based on certain assumptions made within the model used to give you the forecast. The trouble with this type of reasoning is that they are discounting or redefining what is actually an expenditure. In other words, they separate investing from spending and do not consider it an expenditure.

Sometimes, these forecasts are presented as fact, and herein lies the problem. It's like the used car salesman telling you he will sell you a car worth $20,000 for $15,000, thus saving you $5,000. In reality, you just spent $15,000. Spending is spending, regardless of what bucket, account, or subaccount the money comes from. Back home, we would say, "That dog won't hunt."

We definitely need to be good stewards of our resources, and that's why I'm mentioning it here. We also need financial models to give us good information in order to make well-informed decisions. Without them, you're simply guessing. I am just saying that we need to be honest about it.

> *The trouble with this type of reasoning is that they are discounting or redefining what is actually an expenditure.*

Whether you are investing or spending, it's still spending, which carries risk. The goal is to decrease the risk as much as possible, and this is where the models and assumptions come into play. Risk is hard to measure and is even harder to predict accurately. I do not believe it can be accurately predicted. It is an inexact science, and that's why it is called risk. Scientific principles, on the other hand, replicate the same results every time they are tried. Risk does not.

What analysts are really doing is taking a known (money) and applying it to an unknown (risk) to give them a forecast based on assumptions in hopes of realizing a future increase in revenue or gain (profit). What if the assumptions and forecast are wrong? One only has to look at the 2008 stock market crash to realize this possibility.

Let's look at it another way so we can draw a parallel. You could compare financial analysts to a weather forecaster trying to predict the path of a tornado. These weather forecasters use very sophisticated models, which can give a general direction (forecast) of the tornado's path, but that's about all the models are good for in terms of accuracy. In reality, the only one that actually knows where it is going is the tornado. So, if you were going to bet, would you bet on the forecaster or the tornado? I don't know about you, but I'd bet on the tornado every time!

In business, we don't have the luxury of betting on the tornado, so we have to do the best we can by avoiding its path, thus reducing our risk of being negatively affected by it. Some say that you can justify anything you want, given the right numbers and model. That may be true, but that's a discussion for another time.

Sometimes, you have to have faith in those with whom you choose to surround yourself. The message here is to choose wisely, my friends! The name of the game is to make sound decisions with the best information available in order to decrease your risk, based on the probabilities certain models give you. Either way, you're still rolling the dice.

How does this relate to staff development and the workplace environment? Employee-related expenses are given, so you're actually taking money and applying it to a known situation with known risks instead of to an unknown situation with unknown risks. You have greater influence over this type of known situation and its returns than the other.

According to the studies mentioned previously in this chapter, many leaders and employees agree low performance can be attributed to the lack of training and development. Knowing this, one could argue that leadership would be making a conscious decision not to meet their own expectations if they do not provide the resources to do so.

If we truly believe our employees are the lifeblood of our businesses, we should make sure the resources are there to keep them learning and growing. I do not think you can grow your business without growing your employees. The two are inextricably linked. People and their performances equal the level of quality.

> *Employees are and will always be your competitive edge. It is your employees through which your customers interact, directly or indirectly, according to the products they purchase or the services you render.*

Organizational structure can play a big part in developing staff, according to how resources are allocated. The resulting culture can also affect the workplace environment, depending on the dynamics within that structure. Employees are and will always be your competitive edge. It is your employees through which your customers interact, directly or indirectly, according to the products they purchase or the services you render. Your competitiveness is directly related to the quality of the people you hire and develop. Again, the key word here is *develop*.

Not all staff development is monetarily based or driven. The same could be said for the workplace environment. These two (employees and workplace environment) are also inextricably linked. Much of staff development will depend on your efforts to coach and mentor through the building of effective relationships. You, as a manager and leader, impact this greatly.

Resources are important, but the type of investment I am talking about is not a monetary one but one of effort, specifically your effort with your employees. With this type of investment, you can spend as much as you want, and it always adds to the bottom line. All it takes is *spending* some time with your employees and *investing* in the relationships needed to create a great workplace environment. You will never have buyer's remorse, and all it costs is some time and effort on your part. It's time well spent.

So, buck the trend, and don't manage by a top-down organizational chart structure. Instead of looking at it from a top-down perspective, change it to a bottom-up one. Regardless of organizational structure or the financial situation, it's about where you place your emphasis. This needs repeating: IT'S ABOUT WHERE YOU PLACE YOUR EMPHASIS.

Place your emphasis on the employees, their development, and your relationship with them. Put your team at the top of your list of priorities. Remember, relationship-building costs nothing but time and effort. Become that foundation (Figure 7.6), and provide your staff with the tools needed to get the job done. By doing so, you'll develop a great workplace environment. When tough times hit, you will have a structure that can withstand the storms.

Next, we'll look at the steps that you will need to take in order to change your culture by using one degree of difference.

CHAPTER 8

Steps to Cultural Change and One Degree of Difference

It can be a daunting task when one tries to change an environment or culture within the workplace. I see many who struggle with this daily. Some have more success than others, but more often than not, even the successful ones eventually hit a road block and become disillusioned by the halting of momentum. This can be difficult to overcome, even in good times. Given the right steps, one can overcome those barriers. In this chapter, we'll explore the five steps it takes to change a culture.

Ah Ha Moment, "Situational Sickness"

The first step to changing a culture is to recognize that it has to be changed. Many people are disgusted with how they are managing but feel absolutely powerless to do anything about it. They are beaten down by the grind, feel hopeless, and lack the energy to fight anymore. They are relegated to simply reacting to problems, and when total burnout sets in, they even stop doing that. They are then stuck in survival mode, doing the minimum to get by in order to maintain some semblance of sanity.

The "Ah Ha Moment" is the moment in time when you decide that you have simply had enough and will not stand for it any longer. It's when you have become totally disgusted with the situation: *situational sickness*.

It is sort of like the drug addict who has hit rock bottom and makes a decision to do something about it. It's an awareness of understanding that things simply cannot continue in their current state or on their current path. It is when your mind says, "Enough is enough!" It's you making a last stand. The sad part is many never make the stand, and they simply leave.

The greater the despair, the greater the transformation. Situational sickness can provide the motivational energy to make the necessary changes. This will enable you and your organization to break free from the sorry state of affairs you find yourself in.

Once you make the decision to stand, fight, and commit to the path of recovery, you'll experience a feeling of liberation and energy that will surprise most people. You will also feel a peace of mind that had been absent during the turmoil. You will have faced your adversary, been honest with yourself, and come clean with what needs to be done.

It will give you a sense of control over your own fate. It will empower *you* because *you* now realize that *you* and *you* alone will determine how *you* will respond to whatever adversity **you** are facing. This will give you that peace of mind that brings clarity of thought and hopes for a better tomorrow. In turn, this will supply you with the energy to start building that better tomorrow. Is that one degree of difference becoming clearer? Let's continue on!

QBQ Moment, "What Can I do?"

I named this step after John G. Miller's book, *QBQ! The Question Behind the Question.* The question is simple yet so powerful. As previously discussed, this was when I had the blinders taken off, and it was revealed to me where the problem was and who needed an overhaul. I also realized that I was the answer to my problems.

We talked a moment ago about the "Ah Ha Moment" and how liberating and empowering it was and why it gave you that feeling. The *QBQ* moment channels that energy into action by focusing you on the steps required to bring about the change you desire for you and your workplace. It takes the old saying, "The buck stops here," and rephrases it to say, "The buck *starts* here."

> *It takes the old saying, "The buck stops here," and rephrases it to say, "The buck starts here."*

The thing I like about this question is that it demonstrates leadership through personal accountability. Growing up poor, I had every opportunity to explain away my faults and excuse my failures. I could've blamed anyone and everyone. At the time, I didn't appreciate that my poverty forced me into a "No Excuse" philosophy of living. This meant failure was not an option for me.

If I wanted to dig myself out of the poverty I was in, I would have to look at myself (with God's guidance) as to what I could do to improve my lot in life. I had forgotten and lost that for a while until I read *QBQ*. Success had colored my thinking into one of entitlement, and I had forgotten the basis of how my success was built. Mr. Miller, thank you for waking me up!

When you ask yourself the question, "What can I do to make the situation better?" you will start to focus on the steps to take in order to regain control of your circumstances. You will develop an action plan.

Focus first on the process—not on the results. Repeat it again with me, and say it out loud: "FOCUS ON PROCESS FIRST—NOT ON RESULTS." Why is this? By focusing on process, you will stay focused on the steps you've developed to reach the desired results. Most people make the mistake of focusing on the end result and fail to pay attention to the details needed to pull it off. Customer service guru and motivational speaker, Lou Heckler, stated that excellence begins with paying attention to minor details. Pay attention to details because they will make or break your plans. John G. Miller writes,

> The idea that we are accountable for our own choices and are free to make better ones is fundamental to the QBQ. Sometimes, people think they have no choice. They'll say things like 'I have to' or 'I can't.' But we always have a choice, always. Even deciding not to choose is making a choice. Realizing this and taking responsibility for our choices is a big step toward making great things happen in our lives.[1]

Now, we'll turn our attention to commitment, which is the sincerity of belief. This will be the most important part of your decision to change your current circumstances.

COMMITMENT – SINCERITY OF BELIEF

Legendary football coach, Lou Holtz, once said, "The kami-kaze pilot who flew 50 missions was involved; he wasn't committed." Commitment is "the state of being bound emotionally or intellectually to some course of action."[2] Sincerity is defined as "presenting no false appearances."[3]

These two facets of your decision make up what Andy Andrews refers to as a "decided heart." He describes a "decided heart" this way: "A decided heart has to do with how we make decisions and our conduct after that decision is made; it has nothing to do with action or persistence."[4]

Who will believe in you or your vision if you do not believe in it yourself?

You may recognize this quote from the front of this book: "To change a culture, an attitude or an environment, one has to have a vision, a belief in that vision, and a commitment to act upon that belief. Only through a sincerity of change that comes from within will a true commitment to that action produce the desired change." I have found no better way to say it. Let's take a look at a couple of the key words and phrases from the aforementioned quote:

"Belief" – you have to believe in what you are doing. Who will believe in you or your vision if you do not believe in it yourself? Belief produces the "sincerity of change" that you experience within yourself. Belief without sincerity is simply symbolism over substance. Politicians and valueless leaders practice this day in and day out. They are guided by a valueless system of offering up words of hope without action in hopes of persuading you to follow their lead. It is called manipulation, the ends-justify-the-means type of behavior we see so often demonstrated by those in positions of leadership. These are the people who can explain away everything except their own failure. They lack humility.

The next key phrase is "true commitment." Belief combined with sincerity produces "true commitment." Without it, people will not follow. They will sniff out your insincerity as quickly as you can sniff out a skunk crossing your path.

The last key phrase is "desired change." You cannot get to the desired results if you do not have a sincere belief and commitment to your plan of action that will transform not only yourself but your workplace environment. This brings us to the next step. Without it, nothing gets done.

ACTION – MOVEMENT WITH PURPOSE

The quote we just finished diagnosing is simply all for naught if we fail to act. Action without purpose is chaos in motion. Decision without action is simply a thought. There are many self-proclaimed "thinkers" who sit on the sidelines, spouting their views on how this and that ought to be done, yet they never take the risk to act and climb into the arena of life!

What produces action? I mean action in terms of providing managerial leadership. You must first have a purpose. Seems simple, doesn't it? If only it was. Purpose is formed through your vision to meet the needs of your staff, your department, and your organization. The key to that vision and to your success is your relationship with those you lead. Frankly, what you need to do here is develop a plan of action and then start implementing it.

Make sure that you do not go too fast. A convoy can only go as fast as the slowest truck if they want to stay together as a team. This means that timelines need to be reasonable. As your staff successfully achieves each milestone on the timeline, you'll start seeing confidence build within them, which will turn into ever-increasing momentum. Success does beget success, but to start with, you need to plan little victories in order to instill that winning attitude. This is a key concept many do not take into account and are left wondering why their initiative failed. As confidence increases, it will help build momentum to achieve success.

> *They key to that vision and to your success is your relationship with those you lead.*

You also need to be held accountable to the timeline. I would recommend having your leadership team hold you accountable. If you do not have one, a committee of employees will suffice. It is very hard and takes extreme discipline to hold one's self to a timeline.

Action is the application of effort. In this case, make sure it's purposeful effort. Do not overanalyze things like some golfers do. They call it "paralysis by analysis." Develop a vision, include your employees and leadership team, don't be afraid to dream, and then make that dream come true! The path of accountability will lead you to the changes you all desire.

No Excuses

Many find this part of changing a culture the hardest. As stated earlier, my poverty growing up after my parents divorced at the age of 12 was a gift that provided me with the motivation to improve my lot in life. I was afforded no excuses and made none. Did it seem harsh at the time? Certainly, it did. Many times, it was very painful. Yet, it provided a work ethic and a drive to improve myself.

Many, especially in today's world, view this type of "no excuse" philosophy as uncaring. They see it as an uncompassionate attitude fraught with a value system foreign to them. These people are seeing a world of need through eyes of compassion which is what we need to be doing. If anything, the world needs a lot more compassion, but here's where they get into trouble and take a wrong turn.

They make the mistake of using that feeling of compassion to cripple the ones they are trying to help. They remove the *work* part of the equation and replace it with *giving*. This fulfills the giver's need to feel and extend compassion, but what does it do over time to the recipient? It takes away their drive, their self-esteem, and their motivation to improve their lot in life. It makes them dependent on the ones giving the compassion. Some never break free from this. Can you really call this compassion? I think not.

Pat Hill, former coach of the Fresno State Bulldogs, was asked why he didn't allow cool zones (fancy fans that blow cool air on players) on his sidelines. He stated, "Give an athlete an excuse to fail, and they will fail." "No excuses" in managerial leadership is to hold yourself and your staff accountable.

As they say in the military, it's about improvising, adapting, and overcoming. It's about doing whatever it takes, morally and ethically, to get the job done. Many people view this as a negative because most managers and leaders use it in a negative way or in a punitive fashion. With staff, focus on positive coaching sessions that build and instill confidence. Set the level of expectations with them, and usually they'll rise to the occasion. Those who don't are your low performers. They will need to be moved out. I know it sounds harsh, but believe me; you're not doing the team or that individual any favors by keeping them around.

> *"No excuses" in managerial leadership is to hold yourself and your staff accountable.*

People who think they live the "no excuse" philosophy tend to come in three types. The first is the person who talks about what they are going to do but never does it. These are the false prophets of the philosophy. They think getting out of the bed each morning to go to work is working hard. For them, it's all about intent with some effort sprinkled in—not results.

How many times have you heard someone explain away their failure like this? "Yea, but I tried." This is a sure sign of someone who believes that "intent" and "effort" are good enough. The problem is that words do have meaning. In general, people judge you according to what you do and whether or not your actions match what you say. The sad part is that these people actually believe they live by this philosophy.

The second type is the one that just does it, sort of like the Nike slogan, "Just do it." They see a need, step up to the plate, and get it done. These people tend to be very independent and industrious, but their lack of communication can lead to problems. They are results-oriented and driven. With them, the bottom line is all about results.

These people typically will go over, under, around, and even through whatever or whoever they need to in order to get things done. When appropriately channeled, these individuals can be extremely valuable to the team. Leaders who use this method wreak the same chaos and havoc as do employees, but they do it on a larger scale.

The third group is made up of those who tell you what they are going to do and actually do it. In today's world of moral relativism and situational ethics, these people are definitely in the minority. Throughout history, entire political movements have arisen due to people's frustration with their leaders over what they say they are going to do versus what they actually do. As a movement, integrity is foremost in their minds. They watch what people do to see if their actions match what they said they would do.

Employees are no different. As their frustration rises due to an inconsistency between their leaders' words and actions, the leaders' lose the ability to influence, which is the essence of leadership. We know this consistency or inconsistency between words and actions either produces credibility or the lack thereof. Make sure your words match your actions.

The best of the three is the one who communicates what they intend to do and then does it. Employees will not only believe what they perceive, but they'll also believe what they see. When words are matched with actions, credibility is born. Be a person of action immersed in a philosophy of "no excuses," and you'll soon see things getting done and problems getting solved. People will enthusiastically follow a leader with such credibility. Why? They will not only be seen as a person of credibility but also as one of integrity. People are longing for this type of managerial leadership!

When you start from a position of no excuses, things get done. All great leaders know it, great coaches know it, and the managers and leaders I admire most know it.

> *When words are matched with actions, credibility is born.*

By now, I guess you've figured out what that one degree of difference is, so I'll leave you with the quote we started with in Chapter 7—but with a twist:

"If you can't change the people, then change the person, and that person is you."

You are that one degree of difference!

ONE DEGREE OF DIFFERENCE

Never sell yourself short on the influence you exert upon those you lead. Earlier, we talked about a staff or team being a reflection of their coach or leader, and I believe this is absolutely true. If that is true, why do so many leaders find it so hard to change their workplace environment or culture? I believe the answer lies not so much in knowledge but in ability. Don't get me wrong; knowledge is important, but bear with me for a moment, and let me explain.

What I am talking about here is the difference between knowledge, skill, and ability. Skill is related more to learning, gaining knowledge, and the application of that knowledge. You first must learn in order to obtain a skill. You are not automatically born with skill. Knowledge and skill are related, but they are not the same thing. Knowledge may give you the information about what needs to be done without a clue as to how to actually do it. Skill is not only knowing what to do but also how to do it, when to do it, and the ability to do it.

Ability is related to doing, or we could say, performing. Ability is about applying knowledge and skills. In order to develop skills, you first have to apply what you have learned. The degree to which one can apply that knowledge determines skill level. Experience comes from successive application, which allows you to become more proficient and skillful in what you are doing. What I have found is that most managers and leaders lack ability and not necessarily knowledge or skill. They know what should be done, but for some reason, they just can't or won't do it. It could be that the lack of self-confidence causes one not to act, but I think the answer lies a little bit deeper. The inability to do something when the knowledge or skill is present is related directly to motivation. Lack of motivation then becomes an issue of desire, which leads to a lack of commitment. Before you know it, you're in a vicious cycle of a negative, self-fulfilling prophecy.

Remember the quote about the kamikaze pilot who was involved but not committed? He had the knowledge and skill to fly the plane into a ship, but he lacked the desire or commitment to do so. These two elements (desire and commitment) have to do with motivation, and that brings us back full circle to the first step in cultural change: the "Ah Ha Moment."

I am convinced that one cannot change an environment or provide the leadership to change that environment if that individual is not motivated to change it. That motivation must come from within and must arise from a willingness to change one's self. It all starts with the leader. You set the tone and degree of change or transformation.

> *I am convinced that one cannot change an environment or provide the leadership to change that environment if that individual is not motivated to change it.*

The "Ah Ha Moment" is based on hitting rock bottom. I refer to it as "Situational Sickness." This rock bottom or degree of despair is related directly to the degree of transformation. It is also related directly to the degree of motivation. Once people realize how they can change their own performance by learning new skills, applying those skills, and making better decisions, they'll learn how to change their workplace environment. This is diagramed in Figure

5.1, "The Performance Improvement Cycle," and in Figure 5.2, "The Personal Change Cycle."

All we have talked about in this chapter is *choice*. Leo Tolstoy once said, "Everyone thinks of changing the world, but no one thinks of changing himself."[5] It's all about transforming **yourself**, transforming **your** staff, and transforming **your** environment. We are talking about a personal choice, that "One Degree of Difference." It is that simple, and it's your choice!

CHAPTER 9

A VALUED TEAM MEMBER PHILOSOPHY

In this closing chapter, we will explore how to cultivate an environment of approval through a "Valued Team Member Philosophy." Charles Schwab stated, "I have yet to find the man, however exalted his station, who did not do better work and put forth greater effort under a spirit of approval than under a spirit of criticism."[1] You get to an environment of approval through a Valued Team Member Philosophy.

Let us first look at what an environment of approval means, and then we'll define a Valued Team Member Philosophy and its components for both staff and leadership.

ENVIRONMENT OF APPROVAL

What does an environment of approval really mean? Many would say it means acceptance. Let us look at acceptance versus approval. Acceptance can be defined as a "favorable reception."[2] Approval can be defined as "favorable regard."[3] The key terms here are "reception" and "regard."

Reception means "to receive."[4] Regard means "to observe closely or look at something in a particular way."[5]

For example, "We *received* your application for hire." This is based on a process. Acceptance is an act and is process-driven.

"I *regard* him as a hard worker." This is based on performance. Approval is observance and is performance-driven.

Let's put it this way. An employee is accepted when he or she is hired, right? You went through a *process* of interviewing prospective employees and then *acted* on your criteria to offer a job to an individual. Approval is based on the person's performance. At my former place of business, we utilized a 90-day probationary period to monitor a new employee's performance. If they did not meet our standards of performance, they were released. This made the probationary period a crucial time for both the employee and the employer.

Let us delve into this a little further for those who still need a bit more convincing. Say you were remodeling your house. You put the job up for bids and got estimates from several companies. You did all of your background checks and even called the Better Business Bureau. After you finished your process and reviewed all of the bids, you hired a company to do the remodeling. You *accepted* them to do the job.

After several months, they finished the job, and it was a job well-done. You then *approved* of the job they did. What if you didn't approve of the job they did after you accepted their bid? Say their attitude was terrible, and they kept messing things up, not living up to the agreement and your standards for quality of work. You would have then disapproved of the job that they had done.

We have now established that an environment of approval is based on performance and not acceptance. If this is not the case, why would you hire someone for acceptance and not performance?

As I said earlier, acceptance is a component of the culture of approval, but it is not the key factor. It is key and crucial in the hiring process in the sense that you hire the right type of people. It is not key after an individual is hired. It is all about process before they are hired and performance after they are hired.

> When we focus on the positive, the employee will feel accepted by the approval of their performance.

In nursing, approval was based on standards of care and the delivery of that care. As we previously stated, hiring the right people is a crucial component to building a successful team. The key after they are hired is performance, and it can be viewed in a positive or negative manner.

We need to focus on the positive side of performance instead of harping on the negative. After all, their performance is related to your performance as a coach, manager, and leader. I know that hurts, but it's true. When we focus on the positive, employees will feel accepted by the approval of their performance. This is where "On-Time Coaching" as part of "Performance-Based Coaching" is critical.

Remember when I shouted to "FOCUS ON PROCESS AND NOT RESULTS" back in Chapter 8, referencing the *QBQ* moment? Let us take a look at why this is so important in the context of a culture of approval based on performance.

Results-driven performance is short-sighted and concentrates on immediate success. Process-driven performance concentrates on making sure the correct steps are taken for long-term success. You could sum it up like this:

Process-Driven - Seeks Long-term Success
Results-Driven - Seeks Immediate Gratification

In other words, you will never get the results you want by focusing on results because by doing so, you'll not be focused on the steps required to achieve the desired results. On the other hand, by focusing on the process, you will be sure to focus on the steps required to achieve the results you desire.

> *When process becomes second nature, true success is achieved, and you obtain your targeted results.*

Process-driven performance helps the employee build the foundation and confidence for continued success. By focusing on process, it keeps the employee paying attention to detail, which is the basis for excellence. When process becomes second nature, true success is achieved, and you obtain your targeted results. This is what we all want and desire. Results are important, but they are not as important as the process. Without process, you have no results—at least, not the type you desire.

I was watching a replay of the Sunday round of the 2010 Master's Tournament. It was won by my favorite golfer, Phil Mickelson. There came a critical moment in the tournament on hole #13 where Mr. Mickelson had driven his ball through the dog leg. His ball came to rest upon pine straw behind two trees.

Anyone who has seen him play knows that he is not afraid to try any type of shot. After looking at the situation, he noticed he had a three-foot opening between the two trees in front of him. To hit the shot and actually pull it off meant he would have to hit the ball through that three-foot gap off of pine straw while carrying his ball 207 yards over a creek that fronted the green. To make a long story short, he hit one of the greatest shots in golf to within three feet of the pin. It catapulted him to win his third Master's tournament and once again adorn the green jacket for which the tournament is known.

How did he pull off that shot while being under so much pressure? Do you think he was focused on the result or on the process? I'm here to tell you that the result never entered his mind. He was totally dedicated to the process. One only had to watch how he sized up the shot to realize that he was going through the steps he would have to take in order to succeed. He knows, like all great athletes, that in order to perform under pressure, you cannot focus on the result. It's all about the process.

Brad Faxon is widely considered to be one of the greatest putters in golf history. When asked about his legendary success as a putter, he answered that he totally focuses on the process and not on the result.

Now that we have established that a culture of approval is performance-based, you need a process in order to transform your workplace environment. That process is the philosophy of transformational management and leadership contained in this book. The "Valued Team Member Philosophy" is an important part of that process.

VALUED TEAM MEMBER PHILOSOPHY

This was part of a new philosophy I brought with me when I was hired as the manager and leader for our Medical-Surgical Intensive Care Unit. It was born out of my own transformational experience that you read about earlier.

Once explained to my leadership team, they totally bought in and helped build upon it, which made it *our* philosophy. It united us as a leadership team, and their buy-in helped set the stage for an amazing transformation. The results of that transformation can be found in the epilogue.

Just what is a "Valued Team Member Philosophy?" It can be defined as "an agreement between leadership and staff to improve the workplace environment for the betterment of X, with X representing what you are trying to accomplish."

In our case, X represented patient care. We made an agreement with our staff that we would work together to improve the workplace environment for the betterment of patient care. In your case, it could be working together to manufacture better tires, give better service, and the list could go on and on.

This agreement is defined by certain behaviors and responsibilities that are classified as "valued" and "non-valued." Both sides, meaning employees and leadership, agree to focus on behaviors that are valued. This sets the stage for that environment of approval we discussed earlier in this chapter.

Before we get into the actual expectations and behaviors, let's look at the basics of what it takes to be a "Valued

Team Member." What does it mean to add value? Most of the responses I got from our staff centered around worth. *Valued* means "highly regarded" or "much esteemed."[6] So, they were right on the money!

We then need to look at what it takes to be a member of a team. A *team* is an organized group formed for a common purpose.

What does it take to become a member of a team? Some may say you need to join and be accepted in order to be a part of a team. This is true, but it's more basic than that. Let that percolate for a moment, and let us look at the definition of a *member*: "belonging to a group or organization."[7]

> *The basic trait or ingredient necessary for all of this to occur is that the employee has to show up — not only show up but also have a good attitude! This is how they add value and become a part of the team.*

The basic trait or ingredient necessary for all of this to occur is that the employee has to show up — not only show up but also have a good attitude! This is how they add value and become a part of the team. You cannot add value by not showing up. You cannot be a member of a team if you do not show up. By definition, in order to be a part of something, you are required to show up! That is a truism of life. I know it's basic, but it is the cornerstone of a "Valued Team Member Philosophy."

You would be surprised how many employees see absenteeism as a given and as leadership's problem. They say things like, "Well, I wouldn't call in so much if they would provide a better place to work," or, "They'll never miss me.

They'll just get someone else to do it." Leaders can propagate this mentality by the way they treat their employees. If you have ever watched the show, *Undercover Boss,* you have seen how these top-level executives have their eyes opened wide when they go undercover to get the perspective from the frontline employees. I simply love that show.

To summarize, the "Valued Team Member Philosophy" is based on an agreement between employees and leadership to focus on behaviors that will add value to the workplace environment. Both sides agree to focus on behaviors that are valued. This is important, and it's a two-way street. Remember, your behavior affects and influences your staff.

The agreement is crucial for a couple of reasons. The first is that it gives both sides a singular purpose, and the second is that it gives both sides a singular focus. The purpose is your desired result, which is a transformed workplace environment. Your focus is the process in which to get there (i.e. expectations, attitudes, and behaviors). One cannot happen without the other. For example, we'll lay out what our department decided were valued and non-valued expectations and behaviors for both employees and leadership.

Employee-Employee Expectations and Behavior

<u>**Valued**</u>	<u>**Non-Valued**</u>
• *Positive Attitude*	• *Negative Attitude Complaining*
• *Teamwork*	• *Cliques*
• *Professionalism*	• *Not a Team Player*
• *Show Up to Work*	• *Lack of Professionalism*
• *Initiative*	• *Absenteeism*
• *Respect*	• *Lack of Initiative*
	• *Talking Down to Teammates*

Figure 9.1

Figure 9.1 represents the expectations our employees had for their fellow teammates. As you can see, your valued behaviors are in direct opposition to your non-valued behaviors. It is very important that you capture and list these expectations of attitudes and behaviors for all to see. Do it to set the expectation of what it means to be part of a team, and add value to that team. Do this for both employees and leadership.

Now, let us look at the focused attitudes we wanted from our employees.

Employee-Focused Attitudes

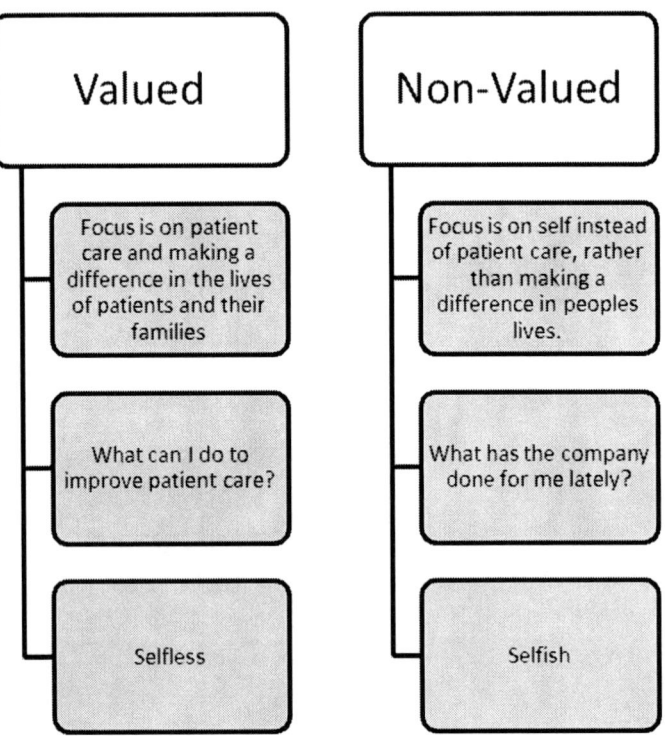

Figure 9.2

As we see in Figure 9.2, you can insert the attitudes that your company values. Let me give you a little hint as to what the three boxes represent.

The first box is focused on the purpose of the employee.

The second is focused on what the employee can do to improve their purpose. It could be, "What can I do to make better tires?" or "What can I do to improve the quality of our product?" This helps them focus on their performance. It also helps empower them with personal accountability and to make better choices as John G. Miller points out in his magnificent book, *QBQ*. Actually, the question comes directly from the QBQ philosophy.

The third box is focused on the appropriate attitude we wanted exhibited by the employee.

Let's turn our attention to leadership and management in terms of their valued and non-valued behaviors.

Leadership/Management Expectations and Behavior

Valued

- *Provide an Environment for Success*
- *Show Concern*
- *Acknowledge*
- *Affirm*
- *Add Value*
- *Performance-based*
- *Coaching*
- *Educational Opportunities*
- *Consistency*
- *Committed to Philosophy*

Non-Valued

- *Poor Environment*
- *Lack of Concern*
- *Never Acknowledge or Affirm Worth of Employee*
- *Punitive or Negative Feedback*
- *Lack of Educational Opportunities or Personal Growth*
- *Lack of Consistency or Commitment*

Figure 9.3

As we look at the behaviors developed for our leadership team, we see the areas of focus. The main focus is on providing an environment where the employee can succeed. That is our responsibility as leaders. It is employee-focused and employee-driven. By focusing on our employees and helping them succeed, the overall organization will succeed. This is true whether it is in healthcare, the service industry, or manufacturing. It lays the foundation for a great transformation to take place.

We'll now look at leadership-focused attitudes. Again, we'll use my profession of healthcare as an example, but it can be applied to any type of organization or industry. These attitudes will shed a light on our motives as leaders.

Leadership- and Management-Focused Attitudes

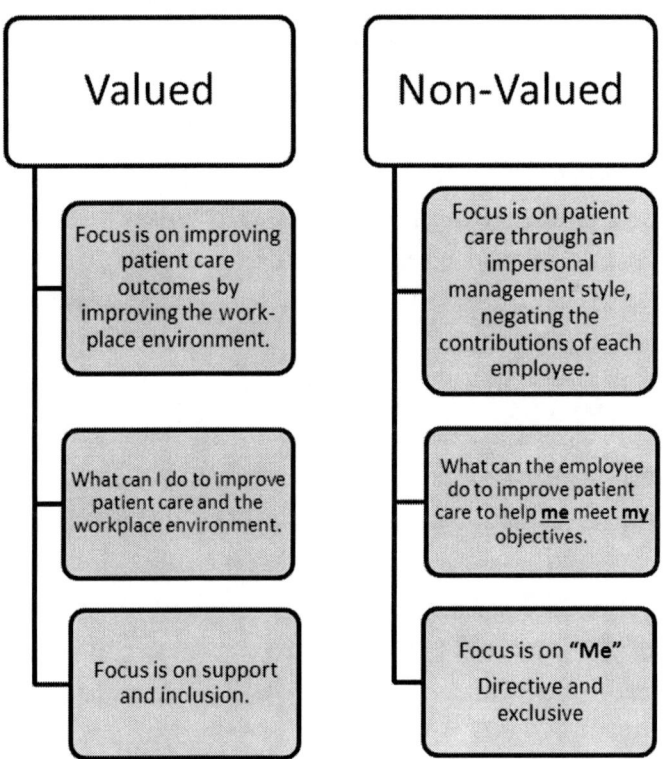

Figure 9.4

From the behaviors listed in Figure 9.4, you can see that the focus is on improving whatever the purpose of your business is by improving the workplace environment.

The first box under the value column is focused on the workplace environment, which is defined as the collective attitude of the employees. Remember, this also includes the development of the employees, which has a direct impact on their attitudes.

The second box is focused on our now familiar QBQ section of "what can I do to improve that environment?" If you have a leadership team, you may want to use "we" instead of "I" in the QBQ question. If you do use the term "I" when asking the QBQ question in your one-on-one meetings with your employees, be sure to explain that you will extend their expectations of you as their leader to your leadership team. This builds accountability for the leadership team as a whole.

As we'll discuss, this shows willingness on your part to ask them for their input, listen to it, and implement it. The results of this question can be seen in Figure 9.5. The question in box number two leads to box number three's area of focus. It produces a sense of support and inclusion for those you lead. This provides an important contrast to the attitude demonstrated by leadership in the non-valued column.

In the non-valued column, all of the attitudes of leadership are focused on "me." Are you motivated to develop a team, or are you motivated to make yourself look good at the expense of everyone else.

This attitude is directive and lacks input from anyone you lead. It places your emphasis on the employee supporting you for your success instead of on you supporting the employee for their success. Have you ever worked for someone that is represented in the "me" column or in the non-valued column? What did that feel like? Did you feel appreciated or used? Uplifted and inspired or wasted and washed out?

When speaking to the team, be sure to avoid using the terminology of "I" and "you." Instead, use the terminology of "we." This fosters a sense of inclusivity from the employee's point of view. It communicates that "we" are all part of the same team. An attitude of support and inclusion keeps your purpose and focus on the team which is where it should be. After all, you are part of a team; are you not?

> *The "we" attitude helps keep the leader's focus on building a foundation for long-term success whereas the "me mentality" only thinks of immediate results and gratification.*

Leaders who tend to focus on "me" utilize "I" and "you" terminology in their communications with staff. This sets the leader apart from the staff, communicating control and exclusion. As a result, the staff feels excluded. These individuals use manipulation of employees to reach goals for their short-term success. By doing so, they keep themselves looking good to higher-ups, including their bosses, administration, or boards. This is done at the expense of the employee, team, and to a larger extent, the organization.

The "we" attitude helps keep the leader's focus on building a foundation for long-term success whereas the "me" mentality only thinks of immediate results and gratification. They simply want it now and will do everything within their power to make it happen now, regardless of who they have to use. I encourage people to never work for someone like that. The problem is that many leaders embrace this philosophy. They may call it by many fancy names that utilize X strategies, but I call it manipulation, and that lacks integrity, plain and simple.

Let us now take a look at the expectations our employees had for our leadership team:

Employee Expectations of Leadership

- Fair
- Visible, Open, and Approachable
- Feedback
- Hold People Accountable
- Lead by Example
- Consistency

Figure 9.5

These expectations were not listed in any order of priority. If you are wondering, the number one expectation for us as a leadership team, given our situation, was to give feedback and hold people accountable. Fairness was a close second, but all categories rated very high on the employees' list of expectations.

After looking at these expectations, who could argue with them? The employees did not ask for the moon and they didn't expect us to deliver something that was out of our control to give. They were very reasonable. These expectations helped us prioritize our areas of focus and start addressing their concerns. It also helped us begin building that foundation of trust, which began transforming the workplace environment.

You may be asking, "How did I gather all of this information?" The content in Figures 9.2, 9.3, and 9.4 was provided by leadership team. The best way to elicit the expectations listed in Figure 9.1 and Figure 9.5 was through one-on-one meetings with each employee.

Why is it important to meet with them one-on-one? Right away, you are telling them by your actions that you value them and what they have to say. It starts the transformative process. It took me approximately three months to get through my 120 or so employees.

To summarize, I ascertained these responses by asking three simple questions. First, I asked them to share with me their top expectation of me as their manager and leader. I then explained that their expectations of me would be extended to our leadership team. I also requested them to hold us accountable to those expectations. This simple question immediately started demonstrating and modeling the attitudes and behaviors of support and inclusion we've been discussing. It addressed, from their point of view, what our leadership team could do to help transform the workplace environment and improve patient care.

Second, I asked them to name the one behavior they wanted their teammates to bring to work every day, the behavior that would add the most value to our team.

Third, I asked them to name the one behavior they didn't want their teammates to bring to work that would detract from the value of the team.

As you document the responses, you will start to see repeating themes. This will help you develop the categories in which to catalog each response. The reason I say categories is because many people say the same thing in different ways. We decided to take the top five categories. In Figure 9.1, we decided to add a sixth category for the employee: employee expectations. This was done because the count was very close between two of the expectations.

After processing and categorizing the responses, be sure to share all of this information with your staff. All of this information combined makes up your "Valued Team Member" Philosophy. I did it through staff meetings where we explained the philosophy, employee- and leadership-focused attitudes, expectations employees had for each other, and expectations employees had for our leadership team.

We explained how their input from the one-on-one meetings helped develop the expectations that would lay the foundation for transforming our workplace environment. This sharing of information starts setting those expectations within the workplace environment. It places everyone on the same page and marks a new beginning.

During new-employee orientation, we made sure we gave each employee a copy of our "Valued Team Member" Philosophy. We thoroughly discussed each part of it so that we immediately set the expectation of what it would take to become a valued team member.

We also used the employee–employee expectations and behaviors listed in Figure 9.1 to help identify the type of employee we wanted to bring into the team. The employees will tell you the type of person they want to work with by identifying the behaviors they think will add the most value to the team. This is why we gave each team member interview panel participant a copy of the employee-employee expectations and behaviors before each interview session.

By reviewing the list of expectations, it helped keep panel participants focused as they interviewed prospective team members. If they are telling you the type of person and behaviors that would add the most value to the team, why not strive to hire that type of individual?

> *If they are telling you the type of person and behaviors that would add the most value to the team, why not strive to hire that type of individual?*

In the one-on-one meetings I had with the employees, I must say many were not expecting the first question regarding their expectation of me as their manager and leader. Some stated they had never been asked that before. Most, if not all, were surprised. Again, take this time to get to know your employees, their stories, and what brought them to your company. It helps to start building that foundation for the relationship to come.

The meetings were basically self-limiting (10-20 minutes) with only the occasional lengthy one. If you set the expectations and goals for the meeting, keep it relaxed but structured. The employee will oblige with amazing clarity. This process also produces an excitement within the workforce and can kick-start the transformation of your environment.

I started these meetings as soon as I took the position full-time. As word spread, I found staff coming up to me, asking when they were going to have their meeting. This reinforced to me that we were definitely on the right track! You can use these meetings to jump-start your action plan and to build energy for that plan. Inclusion builds energy. Start these meetings when you are ready to transform your workplace. It's a great kick-start to success.

SUMMARY

By implementing a "Valued Team Member" Philosophy, you will be addressing the three critical areas of focus for employees. Remember, they want to be acknowledged, which helps them feel valued. They want to know that their work has meaning, which is affirming. Lastly, they want to add value. By acknowledging them, you'll start to change their perspective. By affirming them, you'll start to change their attitudes. By adding value to them, you'll start to improve their performance.

> Acknowledge = Change Perspective
> Affirm = Change Attitude
> Add Value = Improved Performance

To implement this type of philosophy, you must have the heart of a teacher, coach, and mentor. You can do this by adopting a consistent routine of visiting with staff so that you establish an environment for such change to take place. That brings us back to the three most important steps of the process:

Transform **You**rself
Transform **You**r Staff
Transform **You**r Environment

The one consistent factor in all three areas is you!

I am confident that by consistently modeling these behaviors and implementing this structure, you will start seeing a change in your staff's perspectives, attitude, and performance. It will be a transformational change limited only by the degree to which you desire change.

I am also confident that by implementing this philosophy, you will realize and help your staff to realize that improving the workplace environment is based on the collective attitude of all of those involved. The resulting change in perspectives, attitude, and performance will transform your workplace.

Finally, I am confident—wait, let's rephrase that—I *know* that you will see a dynamic change in your relationship with not only the staff you lead but with everyone you come in contact with, both professionally and personally. You'll now be free from the chains and bondage of your past ego. You will be focused on continual learning to improve your skills and performance. This is where I get excited because now you'll finally get it.

As you improve and get better, everyone and every-thing around you will also! The famous rock band, the Eagles, captured this so eloquently in this line from their hit song, "Already Gone." It states, "So often times it happens that we live our lives in chains, and we never even know we have the key." This will be the most gratifying experience of your life.

I will leave you with one final thought. I have come to the realization that, by and large, people will become what they believe themselves to be. So, dream big, believe in your dreams, and make your dreams come true!

EPILOGUE

I left the Medical Surgical Intensive Care Unit and the healthcare industry in the summer of 2013 to pursue and spread my passion for leadership. I was there full-time for a little over three years. You may be wondering what the end results were of the managerial and leadership philosophy you just read about.

I would like you to read what Michelle Taylor Smith, our Chief Nursing Officer, wrote to me in an e-mail in February of 2013, regarding our staff and leadership team. She asked me to share the following with them:

> My sincere appreciation for all of the accomplishments of the MSICU staff. It is a rare week that I don't receive a note or call from a patient or family recognizing the care received in this unit. Additionally, there are quality measures that reflect the care provided as well. The commitment to the safe and quality care of our patients is consistently evident—and it is with pride that I often share (and brag ☺) on the care and professional practice of the Leadership, Nurses, and support staffs on this unit."

I greatly appreciated her support and uplifting leadership style.

Now, I would like to brag on our team a little to let you know about the good work they did during my tenure with them. We were one of the few units to be recognized system-wide at our quarterly management meetings on multiple occasions for our work with patients, families, and quality initiatives.

In May of 2011, we had a video made about our department titled, "Why We Do What We Do," which highlighted our staff's work with a family during a tragic and difficult time in their lives. Of all of the accomplishments we had, I do believe this was one of the most rewarding moments in my managerial and leadership career. It just doesn't get any better than helping put families back together.

We received Pillar Awards (the hospital system's highest award) for quality in October of 2012 for our work in reducing Central Line Associated Blood Stream Infections and again in March of 2013 for reducing Ventilator Associated Pneumonia down to zero from June 17, 2011 until December 31, 2012. In January of 2013, the Center for Disease Control (CDC) redefined Ventilator Associated Pneumonia, which marked the start of a new era in surveillance.

Two of our employees were recognized as "Employee of the Month" for the entire hospital system (Donna Matheny and Dave Cooper) for going above and beyond their duties to help our patients and families. Another employee (Barbara Richards) was recognized as the "In-Patient Care Giver of the Year." Not bad for a workforce of 10,000 strong!

We had one staff member (Austin Caulder) become a Nurse Manager at one of our sister hospitals. Another one of my leadership team members became Regional Director for one of our health care vendors responsible for hospital relations and education for the southeast. We also had numerous staff members go on to anesthesia school.

We hired good employees, and we moved the bad ones out. We had a philosophy of management, a vision that complemented our hospital's vision, and a leadership team that believed in it. Soon, we had more and more staff believing in it. They began recruiting for us, participating on interview panels, and becoming unit leaders, unit coaches, and clinical advisors. We partnered with another health care facility to help orient their staff to critical care.

As our culture changed, others wanted to come and work with us. We went from a place where few wanted to work to one where weekly or daily I would receive resumes, either by mail or in person. We put the right people in the right places doing the right things. We focused on people, structures, and performance. We developed staff and our leadership team, and we didn't settle for second best. We developed a culture where people would enjoy coming to work to practice their profession, and in doing so, we made a difference in the lives of those we cared for!

I could go on, but in short, we took a unit that was struggling and underperforming, and we turned it into a top-performing critical care unit. This brought us alongside the other critical care areas. Their previous poor performance was not because all of the employees were bad. They weren't. We did what we did because we had a core group of good employees and a leadership team that wanted better. We believed in our staff, we believed in what we were doing, and we believed our best was yet to come. We believed.

I would like to take this time to thank Andrew Schwier, a quality person if there ever was one. I have great admiration for him because he stepped up to the plate when many would not. I'm glad that he chose to stay on and be a positive force in supporting the transformation of the unit. He was a colleague and a confidant, always offering a positive perspective along with sound advice. I will forever be thankful for his embrace and support.

Finally, I would like to recognize my former department (Nursing Administration), which is made up of a bunch of wonderful people who helped me to transform my managerial and leadership style and philosophy. Combined with the staff and leadership team of the Medical Surgical Intensive Care Unit, they enriched my life and career, making this book possible.

My hope and prayer for you is that you will take what you have read and apply it. I think you will find out as I did that your staff is ready and willing to follow your lead.

About the Author

Richard A. Hardy is a graduate of the University of Alabama's Capstone College of Nursing where he obtained a Bachelor of Science Degree in Nursing. He worked for 27 years in the health care industry: 26 years as a registered nurse at Greenville Memorial Hospital, which is part of the Greenville Health System located in Greenville, South Carolina. With over 10,000 employees, it is the region's largest healthcare provider for the upstate of South Carolina and the bordering counties of Georgia and North Carolina.

Having started his career as a staff nurse in the Neuro-Trauma Intensive Care Unit, he went on to have a very successful career in numerous supervisory, managerial, and leadership positions within the organization. Of those 26 years as a registered nurse, 23 were in leadership roles.

Mr. Hardy also had extensive experience working closely with the Greenville County Coroner's office and the Greenville County Medical Examiner. He was appointed to two four-year terms to the Greenville County Medical Examiners' Commission by Governor David M. Beasley and Governor Jim Hodges.

At the time of his departure from the Greenville Health System to pursue his passion for leadership training and equipping, Mr. Hardy was a Tier 1 Manager, the highest managerial level one can attain within their system. He managed a 32-bed intensive care unit with over 100 employees.

It is that body of work and experience that led to the writing of this book and the understanding that managerial leadership, by and large, is often not taught and that many are ill-equipped to face the challenges that successful leadership demands.

ENDNOTES

Chapter 1: A Story of Apathy and Awakening

[1] John C. Maxwell, *Developing the Leader Within You* (Nashville: Thomas Nelson, 2005), 103.

[2] Andy Andrews, *Seven Decisions that Determine Personal Success* (Nashville: Thomas Nelson, 2005) 108.

[3] Andy Andrews, *Mastering the Seven Decisions* Live (Lighting Crown Publishers, 2005).

Chapter 2: What Went Wrong?

[1] John C. Maxwell, *The 21 Indispensable Qualities of a Leader: Becoming the Person Others Will Want to Follow* (Nashville: Thomas Nelson, 2007), 145.

[2] John G. Miller, *QBQ! The Question Behind the Question: Practicing Personal Accountability at Work and in Life* (Penguin Books, 2004), 11.

Chapter 3: Transformational Management

[1] *The American Heritage Dictionary of the English Language* (The American Heritage Publishing Co. and the Houghton Mifflin Company).

[2] *Dictionary.com, Unabridged based on the Random House Dictionary* (Random House, 2014).

[3] Ibid.

[4] Mark Sanborn, *The Encore Effect: How to Achieve Remarkable Performance in Anything You Do* (Water Brook Press, 2008), 131.

⁵ Andy Andrews, *Seven Decisions that Determine Personal Success: The Traveler's Gift* (Nashville: Thomas Nelson, 2005), xx.

⁶ John C. Maxwell and Les Parrott, *25 Ways To Win With People: How To Make Others Feel Like A Million Bucks* (Nashville: Thomas Nelson, 2005), Ch. 3.

⁷ Ibid., 11.

⁸ Ibid., Ch. 5.

⁹ Ibid., 13.

Chapter 4: The 5 C's of Leadership

¹ Andy Stanley, *Enemies of the Heart: Breaking Free from the Four Emotions That Control You* (Multnomah Books, 2006).

² James M. Kouzes and Barry Z. Posner, *Credibility: How Leaders Gain and Lose It, Why People Demand It* (Jossey-Bass, 2001), 28.

³ *The American Heritage Dictionary of the English Language* (The American Heritage Publishing Co. and the Houghton Mifflin Company).

⁴ James M. Kouzes and Barry Z. Posner, *The Truth about Leadership: The No-fads, Heart-Of-The-Matter Facts You Need To Know* (Jossey-Bass, 2010), 21.

Chapter 5: Changing Perspectives, Attitudes, and Performance

¹ *The Edge*, 20ᵗʰ Century Fox, Released September 26ᵗʰ, 1997, 117 minutes.

² Andy Andrews, *Mastering the Seven Decisions that Determine Personal Success* (Nashville: Thomas Nelson, 2008), 5.

³ Ibid.

⁴ Ibid.

⁵ John C. Maxwell, *Developing the Leader Within You* (Nashville: Thomas Nelson, 2005), 49.

[6] Ken Blanchard, *The Heart of a Leader: Insights on the Art of Influence* (David C. Cook, 2007), 31.

[7] Ibid., 33.

[8] Proverbs 16:24, *Life Application Study Bible,* New American Standard Bible, Zondervan.

[9] John C. Maxwell and Les Parrott, 25 *Ways To Win With People: How To Make Others Feel Like A Million Bucks* (Nashville: Thomas Nelson, 2005), Ch 3.

[10] Ibid., Ch 19.

Chapter 6: Transforming Your Environment

[1] David Cottrell, *Leadership… Biblically Speaking: The Power of Principle-Based Leadership* (Cornerstone Leadership, 1998), 117.

[2] John C. Maxwell, *The 17 Indisputable Laws of Teamwork: Embrace Them and Empower Your Team* (Nashville: Thomas Nelson, 2001), Ch. 3.

[3] Martin Yate, *Hiring the Best: A Manager's Guide to Effective Interviewing and Recruiting,* 5th Edition.

[4] Proverbs 11:14, *Life Application Study Bible,* New American Standard Bible, Zondervan.

[5] Ken Blanchard and Gary Ridge, *Helping People Win at Work* (Polvera Publishing and Gary Ridge Publishing, 2009), 101.

Chapter 7: Understanding Performance and Organizational Culture

[1] IDEO – quote was taken from their website in the *"About"* section at 222.ideo.com/about/ under the subsection, *"What We Do."*

[2] Roger Conors and Tom Smith, *How Did that Happen: Holding People Accountable – for Results – The Positive, Principled Way* (Portfolio, 2009), 170-171.

[3] Ibid.

Chapter 8: Steps to Cultural Change and One Degree of Difference

[1] John G. Miller, *QBQ! The Question Behind the Question: Practicing Personal Accountability at Work and in Life* (Penguin Books, 2004), 15.

[2] *The American Heritage Dictionary of the English Language*, The American Heritage Publishing Co. and The Houghton Mifflin Company.

[3] Ibid.

[4] Andy Andrews, *Mastering the Seven Decisions that Determine Personal Success* (Nashville: Thomas Nelson, 2008), 80.

[5] John C Maxwell, *The Maxwell Daily Reader: 365 Days of Insight to Develop the Leader Within You and Influence those Around You* (Nashville: Thomas Nelson, 2008), 123.

Chapter 9: A Valued Team Member Philosophy

[1] John C. Maxwell, *Be a People Person: Effective Leadership Through Effective Relationships* (David C. Cook, 2007), 40.

[2] *The American Heritage Dictionary of the English Language*, The American Heritage Publishing Co. and The Houghton Mifflin Company.

[3] Ibid.

[4] Ibid.

[5] Ibid.

[6] Ibid.

[7] Ibid.

CPSIA information can be obtained at www.ICGtesting.com
Printed in the USA
BVOW05s1006300914

368891BV00001B/4/P